Dubai
VISITORS' GUIDE

there's more to life...
ask**explorer**.com

YAS ISLAND YOUR TICKET TO A WORLD OF MAGIC

FOR MORE INFORMATION VISIT **YASISLAND.AE**
CONTACT US AT **HELLO@YASISLAND.AE**

YAS ISLAND.AE
UNITED ARAB EMIRATES

BEGIN YOUR JOURNEY
OF DISCOVERY

HUGE FUN ON YOUR DOORSTEP

Easy to get to, easy to get around, easy to enjoy. Wild Wadi is all family fun and excitement. Watch the kids shriek and scream their way through the best day of their lives. Book your tickets at **wildwadi.com** or call 04 348 4444

Wild Wadi

W A T E R P A R K
Life. Refreshed.

15 YEARS AND STILL DUBAI'S FAVORITE

"I escaped to another world"

-Soha on Slither's Slides

#LiveToTellTheTale

yaswaterworld.com

Live the ultimate water adventure. Yas Waterworld brings you 45 rides,
slides and attractions worth talking about. So experience the excitement at
the UAE's mega waterpark, then go online and tell your friends you
#LiveToTellTheTale f 🐦

Park opens daily from 10AM

Yas
Waterworld
ABU DHABI

Delivering Better Health in the Middle East

Scope of Services at American Hospital Dubai

- Ablation Therapy
- Anesthesia
- Audiology
- Cochlear Implant
- Cardiac Surgery
- Cardiac Catheterization
- Cardiology
- Cardiopulmonary
- Dermatology
- Diabetes / Endocrinology
- Dietary Counseling
- Endoscopy
- ENT Surgery
- Gastroenterology / Hepatology
- Hematology
- General Surgery
- Internal Medicine
- Medical Imaging

- Minimally Invasive Surgery
- Nephrology / Dialysis
- Neurology
- Neurosurgery
- Obstetrics / Gynecology
- Oncology / Chemotherapy
- Ophthalmology
- Orthopedics
- Pathology & Laboratory
- Pediatrics (Children)
- Pediatric Allergy and Asthma
- Pediatric Surgery
- Primary Care
- Rheumatology
- Sports Medicine/Physical Therapy
- Urology
- Vascular Surgery
- 24 Hour Emergency Service

المستشفى الأمريكي
AMERICAN HOSPITAL
DUBAI دبي

ahdubai.com

RK41590

Call Center +971 4 377 55 00

Dubai Visitors' Guide
ISBN – 978-9948-22-524-9

Copyright © Explorer Group Ltd 2015
All rights reserved.

All maps © Explorer Group Ltd 2015

Front cover photograph: Dubai Creek – Hardy Mendrofa

Explorer Publishing & Distribution
PO Box 34275, Dubai, United Arab Emirates
Phone (+971 4) 340 8805   Fax (+971 4) 340 8806
info@askexplorer.com
askexplorer.com

To buy additional copies of this or any other of Explorer's award-winning titles visit
askexplorer.com. Special discounts are available for quantity purchases.

Welcome...

Welcome to the eighth edition of the *Dubai Visitors' Guide*. Brimming with insider tips on everything from cultural hotspots to 'in' eateries and the best boutiques, this mini marvel has all you need to make the most out of your time in this fascinating desert metropolis.

Dubai is a dynamic city with an iconic skyline and a host of top attractions. From sandy beaches to the world's tallest tower, man-made islands to mega-malls, the City of Gold is just waiting to be discovered – and we've got it covered. Written entirely by local residents, the following pages have been passionately created by the same team that brought you the *Dubai Residents' Guide*. Packed with useful information, our guides are updated every year to help you make the most of your trip.

For more information about Dubai and the rest of the region, plus to find out what's happening when you're in town, log onto askexplorer.com – the UAE's one-stop source for everything there is to know about Dubai and beyond.

There's more to life...
The Explorer Team

       /ask**explorer**

Contents

Essentials — 2

Welcome To Dubai — 4
Culture & Heritage — 6
Modern Dubai — 16
Dubai Checklist — 20
Best Of Dubai — 32
Visiting Dubai — 36
Local Knowledge — 40
Media & Further Reading — 48
Public Holidays & Annual Events — 50
Getting Around — 54
Places To Stay — 64

Exploring — 78

Explore Dubai — 80
Al Fahidi Historical Neighbourhood — 84
Deira & The Creek: Dubai's Port — 90
Downtown & Sheikh Zayed Road — 96
Marsa Dubai & JBR: New Dubai — 102
Festival City & Garhoud — 106
Jumeira: Beachside Life — 110
Palm Jumeirah & Al Sufouh — 116
Umm Hurair: Creekside Adventure — 122

Off The Beaten Track — 126
Further Out — 130
Tours & Sightseeing — 140

Sports & Spas — 144

Active Dubai — 146
Sports & Activities — 148
Spectator Sports — 160
Out of Dubai — 164
Spas — 166

Shopping — 178

Do Buy — 180
Where To Go For… — 184
Souks & Markets — 190
Shopping Malls — 198
Department Stores — 212

Going Out — 218

Dine, Drink, Dance — 220
Entertainment — 226
Venue Directory — 230
Area Directory — 236
Restaurants & Cafes — 246
Bars, Pubs & Clubs — 300

Index — 318

Essentials

Welcome To Dubai	4
Culture & Heritage	6
Modern Dubai	16
Dubai Checklist	20
Best Of Dubai	32
Visiting Dubai	36
Local Knowledge	40
Media & Further Reading	48
Public Holidays & Annual Events	50
Getting Around	54
Places To Stay	64

Welcome To Dubai

Welcome to a city of stark contrasts; of sand dunes and skyscrapers, camels and fast cars, museums and malls. Welcome to Dubai.

Whatever your reason for touching down in this desert metropolis, it's hard not to be captivated by its growth and unshakeable ambition. The world's tallest building is already here, and a slew of architectural wonderpieces and whole new communities are not far behind. Yet underneath the shiny surface there is more to Dubai than cranes and five-star clichés: you'll find Emiratis, expats and sunburnt tourists, all exploring this surprisingly multilayered city.

There are a wide scope of activities, cuisines and adventures to be had, many at prices that you wouldn't expect from the 'seven-star' headlines. Try dining in Arabic street cafes, browsing the souks and haggling for souvenirs to get a sense of local tradition, or sample Dubai's plethora of malls, upmarket hotels and fine-dining restaurants for a taste of its luxury reputation. The emirate caters for all needs, including health needs, thanks to its state-of-the-art hospitals such as the American Hospital (04 336 7777).

Outside the city are a whole new set of landscapes and a more traditional way of life. Seemingly endless vistas of untouched sand dunes are just waiting to be explored, so pile into that Land Cruiser and take a tour. Further out, the east coast of the UAE is a haven for divers and snorkellers, and the

Sheikh Zayed Road skyline

delights of Oman's rugged Musandam peninsula are only an hour or so north.

Over the next few pages, descriptions of the local culture and history should provide context to your trip. Following this is the vital information you'll need to get here and stay in style, plus advice on what to do when you first arrive. Things you really shouldn't miss are elaborated on in our handy Dubai Checklist. The Exploring chapter divides the city up, highlighting each area's best bits, such as museums, galleries and heritage sites. In Sports & Spas, you'll find out what the city has to offer for sports fans, keen golfers and those who simply prefer to be pampered. Shopping is your detailed guide to malls, boutiques and souks, and Going Out will help you manoeuvre your way through Dubai's increasingly impressive maze of restaurants, bars, pubs and clubs.

Growing Trade

In the late 1800s Dubai's ruler, Sheikh Maktoum bin Hasher Al Maktoum, granted tax concessions to foreign traders, encouraging many to switch their operations from Iran and Sharjah to Dubai. By 1903, a British shipping line had been persuaded to use Dubai as its main port in the area, giving traders direct links with British India and other key ports. Dubai's importance as a trading hub was further enhanced by Sheikh Rashid bin Saeed Al Maktoum, father of the current ruler, who ordered the creek to be dredged to provide access for larger vessels. The city came to specialise in the import and re-export of goods, mainly gold to India, and trade became the foundation of the emirate's wealthy progression.

Independence

In 1968, Britain announced its withdrawal from the region and oversaw the proposed creation of a single state consisting of Bahrain, Qatar and the Trucial Coast. The ruling sheikhs, particularly of Abu Dhabi and Dubai, realised that by uniting forces they would have a stronger voice in the wider Middle East region. Negotiations collapsed when Bahrain and Qatar chose to become independent states. However, the Trucial Coast remained committed to forming an alliance, and in 1971 the federation of the United Arab Emirates was born.

Formation of the UAE

The new state comprised the emirates of Dubai, Abu Dhabi, Ajman, Fujairah, Sharjah, Umm Al Quwain and, in 1972, Ras Al Khaimah. Each emirate is named after its main town.

Under the agreement, the individual emirates each retained a degree of autonomy, with Abu Dhabi and Dubai providing the most input into the federation. The leaders of the new federation elected the ruler of Abu Dhabi, HH Sheikh Zayed bin Sultan Al Nahyan, to be their president, a position he held until he passed away on 2 November 2004. His eldest son, Sheikh Khalifa bin Zayed Al Nahyan, was then elected to take over the presidency. Sheikh Zayed is still enormously revered in the UAE and, so far, the country has continued to witness astonishing growth under the leadership of his son, Sheikh Khalifa. With his continued focus on the development of the UAE's infrastructure, economic health and cultural contributions, the country has gone from strength to strength, furthering its international relations, safeguarding its environment and promoting its heritage.

The Discovery of Oil

The formation of the UAE came after the discovery of huge oil reserves in Abu Dhabi in 1958. The emirate has an incredible 10% of the world's known oil reserves. This discovery dramatically transformed the economy. In 1966, Dubai, which was already a relatively wealthy trading centre, also discovered oil. Dubai's ruler at the time, the late Sheikh Rashid bin Saeed Al Maktoum, ensured that the emirate's oil revenues were used to develop an economic and social infrastructure, which is the basis of today's modern society. His work was continued through the reign of his son and successor, Sheikh Maktoum bin Rashid Al Maktoum and by the present ruler, Sheikh Mohammed bin Rashid Al Maktoum.

Culture & Heritage

Despite Dubai being a thoroughly modern metropolis, the emirate is very rooted in its traditions. Culture in Dubai is based on the Islamic customs that deeply penetrate the Arabian Peninsula and beyond. Courtesy and hospitality are highly prized virtues and visitors are likely to experience the genuine warmth and friendliness of the local people – if you meet them, of course (only 15% of the population is Emirati). The rapid economic development over the last 30 years, that was sparked by the reign of Sheikh Zayed bin Sultan Al Nayhan (the 'father of the UAE'), has changed life in the Emirates beyond recognition. However, the country's rulers are committed to safeguarding its heritage. They are keen to promote cultural and sporting events that are representative of the UAE's traditions, such as falconry, camel racing and traditional dhow sailing. Various cultural events take place throughout the year in Dubai, as well as in the neighbouring emirate Sharjah where the Sharjah Art Foundation regularly runs art exhibitions. Generally speaking, Arabic culture, as seen through poetry, dancing, songs and traditional art, is encouraged and weddings and celebrations are wonderfully colourful occasions.

Food & Drink

Most of the Arabic food available is predominantly based on Lebanese cuisine. Common dishes are shawarma (lamb or chicken carved from a spit and served in a pita bread with salad and tahina), falafel (mashed chickpeas and sesame seeds, rolled into balls and deep fried), hummus (a creamy

Heritage Village

dip made from chickpeas and olive oil), and tabouleh (finely chopped parsley, mint and crushed wheat). There are also opportunities to sample Emirati food while in Dubai. The legacy of the UAE's trading past means that local cuisine uses a blend of ingredients imported from Asia and the Middle East. Dried limes are a common ingredient, reflecting a Persian influence; they impart a distinctively musty, tangy, sour flavour to soups and stews. Spices such as cinnamon, saffron and turmeric, along with nuts (almonds or pistachios) and dried fruit add interesting flavours to Emirati dishes.

Look out for *al harees*, a celebratory dish made from meat and wheat, slow-cooked in a clay pot or oven for hours, and *al machboos,* in which meat and rice are cooked in a stock made from local spices and dried limes. Fish is widely used in local cuisine; both freshly caught and preserved. *Al madrooba* is a dish which uses local salted fish prepared in a thick, rich and buttery sauce.

Among the most famed Middle Eastern delicacies are dates and coffee. Dates are one of the few crops that thrive naturally throughout the Arab world and date palms have been cultivated in the area for around 5,000 years. The serving of traditional coffee (*kahwa*) is an important social ritual in the Middle East. Local coffee is mild with a distinctive taste of cardamom and saffron, and it is served black without sugar. It is considered polite to drink about three cups of the coffee when offered.

Muslims are not allowed to eat pork. In order for a restaurant to have pork on its menu, it should have a separate fridge, preparation equipment and cooking area. Supermarkets are also required to sell pork in a separate area. All meat products for Muslim consumption have to be halal, which refers to the method of slaughter.

Alcohol is also considered *haram* (taboo) in Islam. It is only served in licensed outlets associated with hotels (restaurants and bars), plus a few leisure venues (such as golf clubs) and clubs. Restaurants outside of hotels, that are not part of a club or association, are not permitted to serve alcohol.

Shisha

Smoking the traditional shisha (water pipe) is a popular pastime enjoyed throughout the Middle East. There are flavours such as strawberry, grape or apple; it's unlike normal cigarette or cigar smoking as the tobacco and molasses are filtered through water. Shisha tobacco is only available to over 18s as it contains nicotine and can be addictive.

There are rumours shisha will be banned, but no laws as of yet, except that shisha cafes must be 150m from residential areas and can only open from 10am to midnight. Keep reading for some of the best spots.

Religion

Islam is the official religion of the UAE and is widely practised; however, there are people of various nationalities and religions working and living in the region side by side.

In Islam, the family unit is very important and elders are respected for their experience and wisdom. It's common for many generations to live together in the same house.

Muslims are required to pray (facing Mecca) five times a day. Most people pray at a mosque, although it's not unusual to see people kneeling by the side of the road if they are not near a place of worship. The call to prayer, transmitted through loudspeakers on the minarets of each mosque, ensures that everyone knows it's time to pray.

Friday is the Islamic holy day, and the first day of the weekend in Dubai, when most businesses close to allow people to go to the mosque to pray, and to spend time with their families. Many shops and tourist attractions have different hours of operation, opening around 2pm, after Friday prayers.

During the holy month of Ramadan, Muslims abstain from all food, drinks, cigarettes and unclean thoughts (or activities) between dawn and dusk for 30 days. In the evening, the fast is broken with the Iftar feast. All over the city, festive Ramadan tents are filled to the brim with people of all nationalities and religions enjoying shisha, traditional Arabic mezze and sweets. The timing of Ramadan is not fixed in terms of the Gregorian calendar, but depends on the lunar Islamic calendar. During Ramadan the sale of alcohol in most outlets is restricted to after dusk, while shops and parks usually open and close later. In addition, no live music or dancing is allowed. Ramadan ends with a three-day celebration and holiday called Eid Al Fitr, the feast of the breaking of the fast.

While the predominant religion in Dubai is Islam, people are freely permitted to practise other religions. The ruling family has, on numerous occasions, donated plots of land for the building of churches. Christian churches of various denominations have been built in clusters on Oud Metha Road (Map 4 B5) and in Jebel Ali, and there is a Hindu temple in Bur Dubai (Map 4 C2).

National Dress

In general, the local population wear traditional dress in public. For men this is the *dishdash(a)* or *khandura*: a white full length shirt dress, which is worn with a white or red checked headdress, known as a *gutra*. This is secured with a black cord (*agal*). Sheikhs and important businessmen may also wear a thin black or brown robe (known as a *bisht* or *mishlah*), over their *dishdasha* at important events. You'll sometimes see men wearing a brimless embroidered hat (*kumah*), which is more common in neighbouring Oman.

In public, women wear the black *abaya* – a long, loose robe that covers their normal clothes – plus a headscarf called a *sheyla*. The *abaya* is often of sheer, flowing fabric and may be open at the front. Some women also wear a thin black veil hiding their face and/or gloves, and some older women wear a leather mask, known as a *burkha*, which covers the nose, brow and cheekbones. Underneath the *abaya*, women traditionally wear a long tunic over loose fitting trousers (*sirwal*), which are normally heavily embroidered and fitted at the wrists and ankles.

Cross Culture

The Sheikh Mohammed Centre For Cultural Understanding was established to help bridge the gaps between cultures and give visitors and residents a clearer appreciation of the Emirati way of life. It organises tours of Jumeirah Mosque, one of the few in the UAE open to non-Muslims (cultures.ae).

Modern Dubai

The City of Gold has transformed into a thriving metropolis with an iconic skyline and ambitious future plans.

Dubai's rise to prominence has taken place at an astounding pace. Since the discovery of oil in the 1950s, the city has transformed beyond recognition. The pace of development over the past decade or so has been particularly noteworthy, with a near constant stream of announcements for new billion-dollar developments. Despite a slowdown during the global recession, Dubai has transformed into a regional metropolis with its eyes firmly fixed on the future and new projects are constantly being announced. It is appropriate then, that Dubai has won the right to host the Expo 2020, which is also helping the emirate to realise its goal of achieving 20 million tourist visitors by 2020. Both transport and infrastructure projects are now full steam ahead.

People & Economy

There are an estimated 150 nationalities living in Dubai and the population has grown multifold over the past few decades: according to a national census, the population in 1968 was 58,971 – in 2013, it was estimated to have ticked over the 2.1 million mark. Expats make up more than 85% of the population. Nearly 71% of expat residents hail from the Asian subcontinent, many of whom work on the construction of the city's massive skyscrapers that have come to define it, while other expats represent various nationalities from all over the world to make a truly global community. Dubai's economy has been weaning itself off oil dependence for the last few decades. Whereas 20 years ago oil revenues accounted for around half of Dubai's GDP, the hydrocarbons now contribute just a few percentage points. Today, the main contributors include trade, transport, real estate, tourism and finance, with the Dubai International Financial Centre (DIFC) alone contributing around 12.1% in 2013.

What's In A Name?

Dubai is introducing a new address system: the city has been divided into several districts, and each district sub-divided into communities. More than 22,000 Dubai streets will be renamed over the next five years, with the address system featuring the building number, street name, community and district. This replaces the rather confusing system of street numbers.

New communities to be aware of are: Burj Khalifa, which includes Downtown Dubai (and of course, the Burj Khalifa building); and Al Souk Al Kabeer, which includes Al Fahidi Historical Neighbourhood (formerly known as Bastakiya). In other cases, a switch has been made to the Arabic name – the famous Palm Jumeirah can now also be referred to as Nakhlat Jumeira, and you'll also see signs for 'Marsa Dubai' which means 'Dubai Marina'.

'Centre' is also spelled 'center', depending on whether it's the name of a Metro station or a building project. Keep an eye out for Jumeira(h), which can be with and without the 'h'.

Tourism

Visitor numbers to Dubai increased by 10.6% in 2013; there were more than 11 million visitors over a one year period for the first time in its history. In 2014, the online statistics portal Statista estimated that Dubai welcomed 11.9 million visitors.

Dubai International Airport is now ranked the world's second busiest in terms of international traffic and passenger numbers are projected to reach 98 million by 2020. Dubai World Central – Al Maktoum International Airport opened in 2010, in the south of Dubai, near to the Jebel Ali industrial area. It opened for passenger services in the second half of 2013, and will eventually become the world's largest airport, with a capacity of 160 million passengers and 12 million tonnes of cargo per year. Now that Dubai is set to host the Expo 2020, visitor numbers are set to increase even further.

New Developments

There's barely a week that goes by when something from the UAE doesn't claim to be the world's tallest, fastest or most expensive. It's actually a smart way to get the country on the map. The Palm Jumeirah and the iconic Burj Khalifa are two examples of developments that have come to symbolise Dubai, and the world's longest driverless metro provides an alternative way to get around, as does the new tram, which is now up and running. There are ongoing metro expansion plans as well as a project for a regional railway. Several facilities are open at Dubai Sports City (dubaisportscity.ae), while the annual Dubai World Cup is held at Meydan Racecourse. And there'll be lots of new infrastructure for the Dubai Expo 2020.

Clockwise from top left: Meydan Racecourse, Burj Khalifa and Dubai Sports City

Dubai Checklist

01 Ski Dubai

This indoor slope at Mall of the Emirates has 22,500 sq m of snow. There are five runs, a nursery slope, jumps, penguins, and a snow park for kids to play in and even go tobogganing! Lessons are available, and there's a cafe halfway up the piste.

02 At The Top, SKY

A visit to the world's tallest building is a must. Ride the super-fast elevator to the 148th floor's viewing deck, At The Top, Burj Khalifa SKY for panoramic views of Dubai. Alternatively, book a table at At.mosphere – the world's highest restaurant.

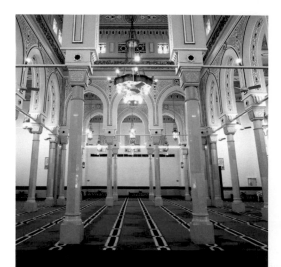

03 Experience Local Culture

Take a tour of Jumeirah Mosque where you can learn about Islam and Emirati culture, experience local hospitality at a 'cultural lunch', or simply kick back, smoke shisha and sample Middle Eastern cuisine at an authentic Arabic cafe.

04 Tackle The Dunes

A trip to the desert is a must during your stay in Dubai. Surfing over dunes in a car at impossible angles is great fun – as is a camel ride, eating your fill at a barbecue and learning how to belly dance. Tour operators are plentiful and professional.

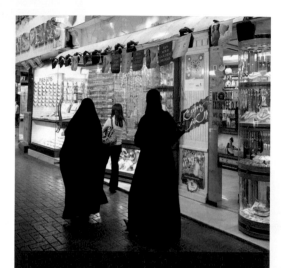

05 Sample The Souks

Still an essential part of life for many people, Dubai's souks are a welcome slice of tradition. Check out the Spice Souk, the colourful Textile Souk in Al Souk Al Kabeer, the Fish Market in Corniche Deira and the world-renowned Gold Souk.

06 Burgeoning Buildings

Splash out on afternoon tea at the Skyview Bar at the iconic, sail-shaped Burj Al Arab hotel.
The other burj, the Burj Khalifa, is the world's tallest building and as such a monument to Dubai's sky-high ambition.

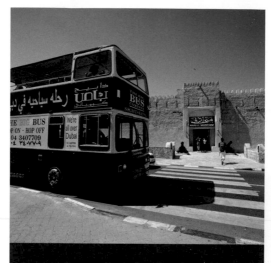

07 Take A Bus Tour

View the city from the upper floor of a double-decker bus, learning some fascinating facts about Dubai along the way. The Big Bus Tours allow you to hop on and off at various attractions, while the amphibious Wonder Bus also takes to water.

08 Hit The Malls

Dubai does shopping bigger and better than most. So whether it's to beat the heat or browse the boutiques, you won't be short of options. Read on for a full guide to the city's shopping hotspots, including one of the largest malls in the world, The Dubai Mall.

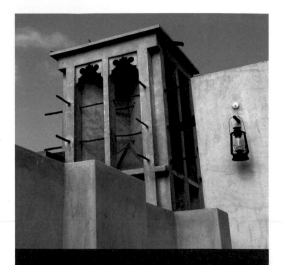

09 Explore Old Dubai

Wander among Arabic windtower houses in the restored Al Fahidi Historical Neighbourhood (formerly Bastakiya). Explore the city's history at the Dubai Museum and learn about traditional trades at the Heritage & Diving Villages on the banks of Dubai Creek.

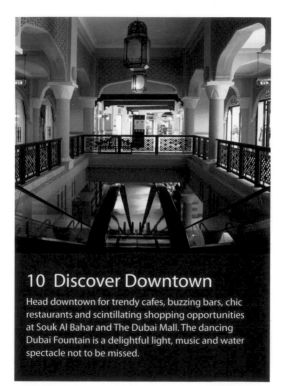

10 Discover Downtown

Head downtown for trendy cafes, buzzing bars, chic restaurants and scintillating shopping opportunities at Souk Al Bahar and The Dubai Mall. The dancing Dubai Fountain is a delightful light, music and water spectacle not to be missed.

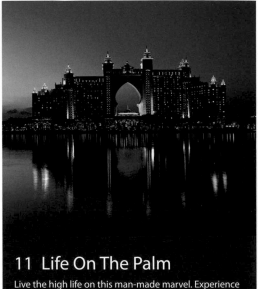

11 Life On The Palm

Live the high life on this man-made marvel. Experience the flamboyant Atlantis hotel with dinner at world-famous Nobu, swim with dolphins, walk through the watery world of the Lost Chambers Aquarium and take the plunge at Aquaventure water park.

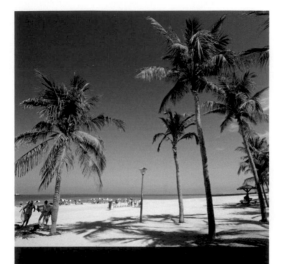

12 Life's A Beach

There's no shortage of sand in Dubai and with kilometres of aquamarine sea beckoning, spending time at the beach is a must. Relax on the golden sands at Jumeirah Open Beach or enjoy exclusive facilities at one of the city's many beachside hotels.

Best Of Dubai

For Adrenaline Junkies

Take a bird's eye view of the growing metropolis while parasailing at one of the many beachside hotels or treat yourself to a helicopter tour.

Dune bashing is a great way to clear the cobwebs and see some spectacular desert vistas. If you go with a tour group, sand skiing or boarding might be on offer too. If you want to get behind the wheel, you'll find dune buggies and quad biking on the road to Hatta. If it's too hot then head to Dubai Autodrome (dubaiautodrome.com) for a karting race around the 1.2km track or the 620m indoor circuit.

To really get your pulse racing, why not take a dip with the sharks at Dubai Aquarium? Novice and experienced divers can take the plunge with the aquarium's 33,000 inhabitants under the supervision of qualified instructors.

For Big Spenders

Dubai is a shopper's paradise offering everything from market stall haggling to haute couture. If labels are your thing, The Boulevard at Emirates Towers is home to several designers but for anything you can't find there try the exclusive boutiques at Wafi. Fashionistas will love the collections along Fashion Avenue at The Dubai Mall where they can rest their heels at the Armani Cafe post-purchase.

For Culture Buffs

Beneath Dubai's glamorous exterior is the Dubai of old. Sample local cuisine, hang out in shisha cafes, explore the souks, travel on an abra, visit the dhow wharfage on the

Fairmont Dubai

Deira side of the creek, hunt for authentic souvenirs, and uncover history at Dubai Museum.

Meanwhile, the art and gallery scene is keeping pace with the skyscrapers. Catch some exciting exhibitions at The Third Line and the jamjar; stay at XVA, a funky gallery and hotel in Al Fahidi Historical Neighbourhood; or visit the galleries at Alserkal Avenue in Al Qouz.

For Foodies

Dubai offers an eclectic mix of American fast food staples, Lebanese street cafes and fine-dining hotel restaurants, but while in town it is the delicious Arabic food that should be top of your list. Try meaty shawarmas, vegetarian falafel, creamy hummus, and fresh tabouleh, all washed down with the finest fresh juices. Try Al Fanar for authentic Emirati cuisine and see our Going Out section for the pick of the rest.

For Water Babies

From relaxing at the hotel pool and Jumeirah Open Beach to diving, snorkelling, sailing and watersports, there are plenty of opportunities to cool off in the water. Make your own mind up in the battle of the water parks, choosing between Arabian-themed Wild Wadi and the Atlantis hotel's hair-raising Aquaventure.

For Architecture Admirers

An architect's playground, Dubai is home to many staggering feats of construction. From the sail-shaped Burj Al Arab to the world's tallest building, the Burj Khalifa, and the teetering towers of Marsa Dubai, there are scores of striking skylines waiting to be captured on camera.

For Party People

Sip cocktails to a Balearic soundtrack as the sun sinks into the Arabian Gulf at 360° or warm up at beach bar favourite Barasti. Trawl the stylish bars of Souk Al Bahar, then dance under the stars at open-sky nightclub Chi@The Lodge, or strut your stuff with the designer set at the Cavalli Club. From the luxurious to the laidback, Dubai's nightlife offerings are surprisingly diverse.

Atmospheric Old Town

The UAE warmly welcomes visitors, but has a few rules and regulations that require extra attention. Read on for the vital information.

Getting There

Dubai International Airport (DXB) handled almost 69 million passengers in 2014. This makes it the second-busiest airport in the world with flights to over 220 destinations. Terminal 1 handles major international airlines; Terminal 3 is exclusively used by Dubai's Emirates; while Terminal 2 is home to budget operator flydubai and other low-cost carriers, as well as charter flights. Terminal 3 has shopping, spas and chill-out gardens. Terminals 1 and 2 are busier, and queuing for check-in and passport control can take a while. The airport is clean and modern, and there's a huge duty free section in Terminals 1 and 3.

Dubai World Central – Al Maktoum International Airport in the south of Dubai opened for passenger flights in 2013, with aspirations to become the world's busiest.

Airport Info

The main phone number for Dubai International Airport is 04 224 5555. For up-to-date flight information call 04 224 5555 and for baggage services, including lost property, call 04 224 5383.

Airport Transfer

If you booked your break through a hotel or travel agency, it's likely that pick-up from the airport will be included.

If not, the metro connects the airport to destinations the length of Dubai directly from Terminals 1 and 3, or you could grab a cab. The taxi stand is straight in front of you as you leave the arrivals hall in all terminals. Taxis leaving from the airport charge an extra Dhs.25 so it costs around Dhs.50 for a journey

Airlines		
Air Arabia	06 558 0000	airarabia.com
Air France	800 23 823	airfrance.ae
American Airlines	04 316 6116	aa.com
British Airways	04 307 5555	britishairways.com
Emirates	600 555 555	emirates.com
Etihad Airways	02 407 2200	etihad.com
flydubai	04 231 1000	flydubai.com
Gulf Air	04 271 6207	gulfair.com
KLM Royal Dutch Airlines	800 556	klm.com
Lufthansa	04 373 9100	lufthansa.com
Oman Air	04 351 8080	omanair.com
Qatar Airways	04 231 9999	qatarairways.com
Royal Brunei Airlines	04 334 4884	flyroyalbrunei.com
Royal Jet	04 505 1777	royaljetgroup.com
Singapore Airlines	04 316 6888	singaporeair.com
South African Airways	04 397 0766	flysaa.com
United Airlines	800 0441 5492	united.com
Virgin Atlantic	04 406 0600	virgin-atlantic.com

to the hotels on Sheikh Zayed Road and the Burj Khalifa area or up to Dhs.90 to Marsa Dubai and the beach hotels of JBR.

An airport bus runs to and from the airport every 30 minutes, 24 hours a day. There are a number of loop routes: C1 runs to Satwa, while the 88 goes to Nakheel Metro Station. Log on to wojhati.rta.ae to plan your journey.

Visas & Customs

Requirements vary depending on your country of origin and it's wise to check the regulations before departure. GCC nationals (Bahrain, Kuwait, Qatar, Oman and Saudi Arabia) do not need a visa to enter Dubai. Citizens from many other countries get an automatic visa upon arrival at the airport (see info box below for the full list). The entry visa is valid for

Visa On Arrival

Citizens of these countries receive an automatic visa on arrival: Andorra, Australia, Austria, Belgium, Brunei, Bulgaria, Canada, Croatia, Cyprus, Czech Republic, Denmark, Estonia, Finland, France, Germany, Greece, Hong Kong, Hungary, Iceland, Ireland, Italy, Japan, Latvia, Liechtenstein, Lithuania, Luxembourg, Malaysia, Malta, Monaco, Poland, The Netherlands, New Zealand, Norway, Portugal, Romania, San Marino, Singapore, Slovakia, Slovenia, South Korea, Spain, Sweden, Switzerland, United Kingdom, United States of America and Vatican City.

30 days, although you can renew for a further 30 days. For those travelling onwards to a destination other than that of the original departure, a special transit visa (up to 96 hours) may be obtained free of charge through selected airlines.

Certain medications, including codeine, Temazepam and Prozac, are banned even though they are freely available in other countries. High-profile cases have highlighted the UAE's zero tolerance to drugs. Even a miniscule quantity in your possession could result in a lengthy jail term. Bags will also be scanned to ensure you have no offending magazines, DVDs or other forbidden items.

Dos & Don'ts

The UAE is one of the most tolerant and liberal states in the region, but as a guest in a Muslim country you should act accordingly. Lewd and drunken behaviour is not only disrespectful but can lead to arrest and detention. There is also zero tolerance to drinking alcohol and driving. Women should be aware that revealing clothing can attract unwanted attention, so very short dresses and strapless tops should be avoided outside of beach areas – though you will see short dresses and skimpy tops in nightclubs, along with those ubiquitous Dubai stilettos. Malls have put up signs making it clear that inappropriate clothing and public displays of affection are not allowed. It is courteous to ask permission before photographing people, particularly women. With prices for cigarettes low, smoking is very common. However, the law states that lighting up in malls and some restaurants is banned, so it's best to check the policy before striking up.

Climate

Dubai has a subtropical and arid climate. Sunny blue skies and high temperatures can be expected most of the year. Rainfall is infrequent, averaging only 25 days per year, mainly in winter (December to March). Summer temperatures can hit a soaring 48°C (118°F) and with humidity well above 60% it can make for uncomfortable conditions from June to September. The most pleasant time to visit Dubai is during the cooler winter months when average temperatures range between 14°C and 30°C, perfect for comfortable days on the beach and long, lingering evenings outside. For up-to-date weather forecasts, see services.dubaiairports.ae/dubaimet.

Time

The UAE is four hours ahead of UCT (Universal Coordinated Time – formerly known as GMT). There is no altering of clocks for daylight saving in the summer, so when Europe and North America lose an hour, the time in the UAE stays the same. Most offices and schools are closed on Fridays and Saturdays. This causes few problems for visitors but be aware that the metro and some shops don't open until later on Fridays.

Electricity & Water

The electricity supply is 220/240 volts and 50 cycles. Most hotel rooms and villas use the three-pin plug that is used in the UK. Adaptors are widely available and only cost a few dirhams. Tap water is desalinated sea water and is perfectly safe to drink although most people choose mineral water because it tastes better. Bottled water is cheap, especially local brands such as Masafi and Arwa. Bottled water, both local and imported, is served in hotels and restaurants.

Money

Credit and debit cards are widely accepted around Dubai. Foreign currencies and travellers' cheques can be exchanged in licensed exchange offices, banks and hotels. Cash is preferred in the souks, markets and in smaller shops, and paying in cash will help your bargaining power. If you've hired a car, be aware that only cash is accepted at most petrol pumps.

The monetary unit is the dirham (Dhs.), which is divided into 100 fils. The currency is also referred to as AED (Arab Emirate Dirham). Notes come in denominations of Dhs.5 (brown), Dhs.10 (green), Dhs.20 (light blue), Dhs.50 (purple), Dhs.100 (pink), Dhs.200 (yellowy-brown), Dhs.500 (blue) and Dhs.1,000 (browny-purple).

The dirham has been pegged to the US dollar since 1980, at a mid rate of $1 to Dhs.3.6725.

Tipping

Tipping practices are similar across hotels, restaurants and bars in Dubai, with tips being shared between all of the staff. Many places add a service charge onto the bill but no one really knows if this actually goes to the staff so many people add a little extra. The usual amount to tip is 10%. Many restaurant bills in hotels automatically come with 10% municipality tax and 10% service charge included, so check the total amount carefully. In a taxi it is standard, but not compulsory, to round up the fare to the nearest Dhs.5.

Language

Arabic is the official language of the UAE, although English, Hindi, Malayalam and Urdu are commonly spoken by residents who have moved to Dubai from Asian countries. You can easily get by with English, but if you can throw in a couple of Arabic words here and there, you're likely to receive at least a smile.

Basic Arabic

General

Yes	na'am
No	la
Please	min fadlak (m)/min fadliki (f)
Thank you	shukran
Praise be to God	al-hamdu l-illah
God willing	in shaa'a l-laah

Greetings

Greeting (peace be upon you)	as-salaamu alaykom
Greeting (in reply)	wa alaykom is salaam
Good morning	sabah il-khayr
Good morning (in reply)	sabah in-nuwr
Good evening	masa il-khayr
Good evening (in reply)	masa in-nuwr
Hello	marhaba
Hello (in reply)	marhabtayn
How are you?	kayf haalak (m)/kayf haalik (f)
Fine, thank you	zayn, shukran (m)/zayna, shukran (f)

Welcome	ahlan wa sahlan
Goodbye	ma is-salaama

Introduction

My name is...	ismiy…
What is your name?	shuw ismak (m) / shuw ismik (f)
Where are you from?	min wayn inta (m) / min wayn (f)

Questions

How many / much?	kam?
Where?	wayn?
When?	mataa?
Which?	ayy?
How?	kayf?
What?	shuw?
Why?	laysh?
And	wa

Numbers

Zero	sifr
One	waahad
Two	ithnayn
Three	thalatha
Four	arba'a
Five	khamsa
Six	sitta
Seven	saba'a
Eight	thamaanya
Nine	tiss'a
Ten	ashara

Crime & Safety

Pickpocketing and crimes against tourists are a rarity in Dubai, and visitors can enjoy feeling safe and unthreatened in most places around town. A healthy degree of caution should still be exercised, however, and most hotels offer safes for keeping your valuables and travel documents locked away.

To avoid a great deal of hassle if your personal documents go missing, make sure you keep one photocopy with friends or family back home and one copy in your hotel safe. Dubai Police will advise you on a course of action in the case of a loss or theft. If you've lost something in a taxi, call the taxi company (see the last page of this book). If you lose your passport, your next stop should be your embassy or consulate (see the pull-out map). With high accident rates, extra caution should be taken on Dubai's roads, whether navigating the streets on foot

Police

Dubai Police's Department for Tourist Security is a helpful, friendly service should you run into any trouble during your stay. For assistance, call the toll free number (800 423) or visit the Dubai Police website, dubaipolice.gov.ae. There's a hotline for reporting problems on the beach, including sexual harassment or annoyance by quad bikes (04 266 1228). For other emergency services call 999 for police or ambulance and 997 for fire.

or in a vehicle. Use designated pedestrian crossings wherever possible (jaywalking is actually illegal), and make sure all cars are going to stop before you cross. There is zero tolerance towards drink driving, even after one pint (there is no legal limit), and if you're caught you can expect a spell in prison. With thousands of low-fare taxis available, there is no excuse or need.

Accidents & Emergencies

If you witness an accident or need an ambulance in an emergency situation, the number to call is 999. For urgent medical care, there are several private hospitals with excellent A&E facilities. The American Hospital Dubai (ahdubai.com) is among the biggest and most trusted – see the pull-out map for listings and contact details. Anyone can receive emergency treatment in government hospitals but note that charges apply to those without Dubai health cards. For general non-emergency medical care, most hospitals have a walk-in clinic where you can simply turn up for a consultation with a physicist; for example, Medcare (medcarehospital.com) has several clinics across Dubai.

People With Disabilities

Dubai is starting to consider the needs of visitors with special needs more seriously although, in general, facilities are limited, particularly at older tourist attractions. When asking if a location has wheelchair access, make sure it really does – an escalator is considered 'wheelchair access' in some instances. That said, Dubai International Airport is well equipped for travellers with special needs, with automatic doors, large lifts and all counters accessible by wheelchair users, as well as several services such as porters, special transportation and quick check-in to avoid long queues. Dubai Transport has a few specially modified taxis for journeys from the airport and around town, and all metro stations are designed to give easy access to wheelchair users. Metro stations also have tactile floor routes for visually impaired people. Most of the newer malls have wheelchair access and recently built five-star hotels should offer accessible rooms for visitors with special needs.

Telephone & Internet

Etisalat offers a visitor pack valid for only 30 days, which costs Dhs.35 for the SIM card and includes 100MB of data, 25 SMS, and 25 minutes of local and international calls. The service can be extended. Alternatively, you can buy du's prepaid Visitor Mobile Line (VML), which costs Dhs.35. You get 20 national or international minutes, 20 national or international SMS, and 200MB of data. du also has a Dhs.55 Pay-As-You-Go plan with 10 flexi minutes (national and international calls), valid

Public Toilets

You will find plenty of clean, modern, western-style toilets in the malls but there is a lack of public bathrooms on shopping streets. Facilities on open beaches tend to be pretty basic, so carrying tissues and hand sanitiser will come in handy.

Deira Creekside

for three days. It comes with international roaming and easy recharge options starting from just Dhs.2. You can buy top-up cards for both packages from supermarkets, newsagents and petrol stations. Mobile phone numbers in the UAE begin with 050, 052, 055 or 056. Wi-fi is available in many hotel rooms. Most five-star accommodation also includes the use of a business centre (sometimes for a fee) with computers and internet access. Many cafes around Dubai offer free wi-fi; some of the hotspots include Starbucks, Caribou Coffee and cafes in Mall of the Emirates and The Dubai Mall.

Media & Further Reading

Newspapers & Magazines

There are several English language newspapers in Dubai. You will see free copies of 7Days on display; this daily tabloid contains international news alongside cinema listings and gossip. The National (Dhs.3), Khaleej Times (Dhs.3) and Gulf News (Dhs.5) are broadsheets that offer local and international current affairs with regular supplements. UK broadsheet The Times publishes an international edition, which is available daily for Dhs.10 in most supermarkets. Larger supermarkets and newsagents also stock copies of international newspapers from the Financial Times and Wall Street Journal to Le Figaro and La Repubblica.

For magazines and lifestyle titles, there are plenty of local options, including a range of Middle Eastern editions of international titles that are produced in Dubai. These include Harper's Bazaar, OK!, Hello! and Grazia for all the regular

More Info?

To find out more about what's going on in Dubai, check out askexplorer. com, Explorer's community driven hub for news, events and local information. For the lowdown on all there is to experience across the whole country, grab a copy of *The Ultimate UAE Explorer* or *Daytripper*. If you fancy getting behind the wheel on the stunning sand dunes, *The UAE Off-Road Explorer* is essential reading. These titles and many more are available at askexplorer.com/shop.

gossip and news, with extras from around the region. Bookshops such as Borders stock a good selection, as do most larger supermarkets. Many of the major, international glossy magazines are also available in Dubai (although as they're imported from the US or Europe, you can expect to pay at least twice the normal cover price). All international titles are examined and, where necessary, censored to ensure that they don't offend the country's moral codes.

Television

Most hotel rooms will have satellite or cable, broadcasting a mix of local and international channels. You'll find MTV, major news stations and some BBC programming, in addition to the standard hotel room information loop. For a slice of local flavour, check out local stations City7, Dubai TV and Dubai One, all of which broadcast Arabic soap operas, talkshows and American sitcoms in addition to local news programmes.

Radio

Catering for Dubai's multinational inhabitants, there are stations broadcasting in English, French, Hindi, Malayalam and Urdu. Daily schedules can be found in newspapers. Of the English-speaking stations, there is a good range to choose from. Tune into Dubai 92 (92.0 FM) for chatty programmes with European music, or try Radio 1 (104.1 FM), Radio 2 (99.3 FM), The Coast (103.2 FM) and Virgin Radio (104.4 FM) for music, or Dubai Eye (103.8 FM) for talk radio and sport. All stations broadcast regular news and travel updates. Sadly, the BBC World Service ceased broadcasting in Dubai in 2010.

Public Holidays

The Islamic calendar starts from the year 622AD, the year of Prophet Muhammad's migration (*Hijra*) from Mecca to Al Madinah. Hence, the Islamic year is called the *Hijri* year and dates are followed by AH (AH stands for *Anno Hegirae*, meaning 'after the year of the *Hijra*'). As some holidays are based on the sighting of the moon and do not have fixed dates on the *Hijri* calendar, Islamic holidays are more often than not confirmed less than 24 hours in advance. The main Muslim festivals are *Eid Al Fitr* (the festival of the breaking of the fast, which marks the end of Ramadan) and *Eid Al Adha* (the festival of the sacrifice, which marks the end of the pilgrimage to Mecca). *Mawlid Al Nabee* is the holiday celebrating Prophet Muhammad's birthday, and *Lailat Al Mi'raj* celebrates the Prophet's ascension into heaven.

In general, public holidays are unlikely to disrupt a visit to Dubai, except that shops may open a bit later and on a few specific days, alcohol is not served. During Ramadan, food and beverages cannot be consumed in public during the day;

Public Holidays

New Year	1 Jan 2015 (Fixed)
Mawlid Al Nabee	3 Jan 2015 (Moon)
Lailat Al Mi'raj	15 May 2015 (Moon)
Eid Al Fitr	18 July 2015 (Moon)
Arafat Day	24 Sept 2015 (Moon)
Eid Al Adha	25 Sept 2015 (Moon)
Islamic New Year's Day	15 Oct 2015 (Moon)
UAE National Day	2 Dec 2015 (Fixed)

however, in most tourist hotels, there are special areas which serve diners all day long. Smoking and chewing gum are also prohibited, and you should dress more conservatively than usual. These rules apply to Muslims and non-Muslims alike.

Annual Events

Throughout the year, Dubai hosts an impressive array of events, from the world's richest horse race and international tennis to well-respected jazz and film festivals. Thousands of international visitors arrive and tickets sell quickly.

Dubai Shopping Festival

January to February

Various Locations   dubaievents.ae

Dubai Shopping Festival is a great time to be in the city with bargains galore for shoppers and entertainers, prize draws and kids' shows held in participating malls.

Omega Dubai Desert Classic

January to February

Emirates Golf Club

Al Sufouh 2   dubaidesertclassic.com

A longstanding PGA European Tour fixture and a highly popular event among Dubai's expat golfing community.

Dubai Duty Free
Tennis Championships

February to March

Dubai Tennis Stadium,

Al Garhoud   dubaidutyfreetennischampionships.com

Firmly established on the ATP and WTP circuit, this major tournament attracts the world's top men's and women's seeds.

Emirates Airline Dubai International Jazz Festival
February

Dubai Media City, Al Sufouh 2   dubaijazzfest.com

The Jazz Festival attracts a broad range of artists from all around the world to a chilled and pleasant setting in Dubai Festival City.

Abu Dhabi Desert Challenge
March

Empty Quarter, Abu Dhabi   abudhabidesertchallenge.ae

This high-profile motorsport event attracts some of the world's top rally drivers and bike riders.

Dubai World Cup
March

Meydan Racecourse, Meydan, Nadd Al Shiba 1   dubaiworldcup.com

The buzzing atmosphere at the richest horse race in the world (total prize money has before amounted to more than $27 million) makes it one of the year's big social occasions.

Seeing Stars

Large-scale concerts and other events attracting top name celebrities are regularly hosted in the UAE. The past few years have seen just about everyone from Kylie to Andrea Bocelli perform live in Dubai or a short hop away in Abu Dhabi. Other fixtures have seen Train, Macy Gray, James Blunt and the late Amy Winehouse strut their stuff, while superstar DJs Fat Boy Slim and Paul Oakenfold have taken to the decks. Check out askexplorer.com to find out what's on when you're in town.

Camel Racing
November to March

Al Marmoom Camel Racetrack, Al Marmoom   meydan.ae

This popular local sport is serious business, with racing camels changing hands for as much as Dhs.10 million. Races take place during winter from 7am to 8.30am. It's quite a sight! Admission is free.

Formula 1 Etihad Airways Abu Dhabi Grand Prix
November

Yas Marina Circuit, Abu Dhabi   formula1.com

Racing fans delight in this F1 weekend; the event usually has a number of big name concerts to top up the experience.

DP World Tour Championship
November

Jumeirah Golf Estates   dpworldtourchampionship.com

The final fixture of the Race To Dubai tournament in which the world's best have a shot at a share of the $8 million prize fund.

Emirates Airlines Dubai Rugby Sevens
November

The Sevens   dubairugby7s.com

Over 130,000 people come to watch top international and local Gulf teams battle it out. With friendly rivalry and prizes for fancy dress, the party carries on until the small hours.

Dubai International Film Festival
December

Madinat Jumeirah, Al Sufouh 2   dubaifilmfest.com

A showcase of Hollywood, international and regional films with screenings in cinemas across the city.

Getting Around

With the expanding metro system, air-conditioned buses and cheap taxis, travelling round Dubai is easier than you think.

You may have heard horror stories about arduous commutes, sticky strolls in the summer and terrifying taxi journeys, but it is surprisingly simple, and pretty cheap, to get around Dubai. Public transport took its first real leap forward in 2009 with the launch of Dubai Metro. Cheap and plentiful taxis are still a popular method of transport, but don't overlook the even cheaper bus routes; it's even possible to explore some areas on foot during the cooler winter months. If you prefer to be in control then hiring a car is a great way to get out of the city but bear in mind the variable driving standards of many motorists. If you're keen to get off the road then take a trip on a traditional abra or modern water bus. Many people use them for daily trips and they offer a fresh perspective on the city.

Metro

Dubai's driverless metro currently has two lines. The Red Line, which runs from Rashidiyah to Dubai International Airport, and down Sheikh Zayed Road – passing the financial district, Burj Khalifa, Al Barsha and Marsa Dubai – before terminating at Jebel Ali. The Green Line runs from Al Qusais on the Sharjah border to Jaddaf. Most of the stations along the existing lines are now open – check dubaimetro.eu for updates. Blue, Gold

Dubai Metro network

and Purple Lines are planned to be running by 2030 and the current Red and Green Lines will be further expanded.

Trains run from 5.50am to midnight Saturday to Wednesday; 5.50am to 1am on Thursdays; and 1pm to 1am on Fridays. The frequency is every 3.45 minutes during peak times, and every seven minutes during off-peak hours. Each train has a section for women and children only, and a first or Gold Class cabin. The fare structure operates as a pay-as-you-go system, in which you scan your prepaid Nol card in and out of stations.

Commuters can also take advantage of du wi-fi at stations and on the trains themselves. Access cards are available for Dhs.20 per hour, or you can pay via credit card at a rate of Dhs.10 per hour.

There is a feeder bus system to transport passengers from stations to local destinations. The buses are free if boarded within 30 minutes of exiting the metro. Each station also has a taxi rank outside the exit to help you reach destinations that aren't accessible by bus.

A monorail runs the length of Nakhlat Jumeira from the Gateway Towers station on the mainland to Atlantis hotel. Trains run daily from 10am to 10pm and cost Dhs.15 for a single fare or Dhs.25 for a return. Dubai's highly anticipated Tram system, designed as a key link for the Dubai Metro and the Palm (Nakhlat) Monorail, was finally unveiled in November 2014. It runs along Al Sufouh Road, linking Mall of the Emirates, Marsa Dubai and Jumeirah Lakes Towers. Commuters pay Dhs.3 to travel across the 11 stations on its route; red ticket holders are charged a flat rate of Dhs.4.

Bus

There are dozens of bus routes servicing the main residential and commercial areas of Dubai. The buses and bus shelters are air-conditioned, modern and clean, although they can be crowded at peak times. The main bus stations are near the Gold Souk in Deira and on Al Ghubaiba Road in Bur Dubai. Buses run at regular intervals until around midnight and a handful of Nightliner buses operate from 11.30pm till 6am. The front three rows of seats on all buses are reserved for women and children only. Cash is not accepted so you need to purchase a Nol card (see below) before boarding. Call the RTA (800 9090) or check the website (rta.ae) for comprehensive route plans, timetables and fares.

Nol Card

Nol cards are rechargeable travel cards which can be used to pay for public transport and street car parking. Single journeys start at Dhs.1.80 for up to 3km, rising to Dhs.5.80 for travel across two or more zones. The red Nol card is a paper ticket aimed at tourists and occasional users. It can be charged for up to 10 journeys, but is only valid on one type of transport at a time – bus, Metro or water bus. The silver Nol card costs Dhs.20, including Dhs.14

Journey Planner

The best way to work out your public transport options is to use the Road & Transport Authority's (RTA) online journey planner at wojhati.rta. ae (*wojhati* is Arabic for journey planner). For further assistance, call the RTA on 800 9090.

credit. It can be recharged up to Dhs.500 and is a better option if you plan to use different types of public transport or travel extensively while in town. The gold card is identical to the silver, except that holders are charged first class prices (usually double the standard fare) and can travel in the gold class cabins of the metro. Nol cards can be purchased and topped up at metro and bus stations and at supermarkets including Carrefour and Spinneys.

Cycling

A lot of care is needed when cycling in the UAE as some drivers pay little attention to other cars, much less cyclists. Also, in the hotter months, you'll be pedalling in 45°C heat. If you are visiting in winter and want to cycle, head to Creek Park where you can rent a bike and explore in safety.

Driving & Car Hire

It's a brave individual who gets behind the wheel in Dubai. Drivers are erratic, roads are constantly changing and the

Car Rental Agencies

Avis	800 2847	avis.ae
Budget Rent A Car	800 2722	budget-uae.com
Diamondlease Car Rental	800 37483	diamondlease.com
EuroStar Rent A Car	04 266 1117	eurostarrental.com
Hertz UAE	800 43789	hertzuae.com
National Car Rental	04 283 2020	national-ae.com
Thrifty Car Rental	800 4770	thriftyuae.com

traffic jams can be enduring. On the bright side, most cars are automatic, which makes city driving a lot easier. If you are a confident driver, you'll probably find that driving in Dubai looks much worse than it is in practice. Expect the unexpected and use your mirrors and indicators. Weekends, especially Fridays, are much clearer on the roads but during the week, traffic heading into Dubai from Deira in the morning and out in the evening can be horrendous. Driving is on the right hand side of the road.

International car rental companies, plus a few local firms, can be found in Dubai. Prices range from Dhs.80 a day for smaller cars to Dhs.1,000 for limousines. Comprehensive insurance is essential; make sure that it includes personal accident coverage. To rent a car, you need a copy of your passport, a valid international driving licence and a credit card. The rental company may be able to help arrange international or temporary local licences for visitors.

Parking is plentiful at most malls and is free for at least the first three hours. Street parking spaces can be hard to find but cost just Dhs.2 for one hour and are free of charge between 1pm and 4pm. You can pay in cash or with a Nol card at ticket machines, or those with a local SIM can pay via SMS. Instructions are posted on ticket machines.

Taxi

Taxis remain a common way of getting around. There are seven companies operating nearly 8,000 metered cabs with a fixed fare structure. All cars are clean and modern, and the fares are cheaper than in most international cities. A fleet of

'ladies' taxis,' with distinctive pink roofs and female drivers, are meant for female passengers and families only. The minimum fare is currently Dhs.10 and the pickup charge from the airport is Dhs.25. It is also possible to hire a taxi for 12 or 24 hour periods. Taxis can be flagged down by the side of the road, or you can order one through Dubai Taxi by calling 04 208 0808. This number is also useful for complaints and lost item enquiries.

Unlike some other cities, there's no 'knowledge' style exam for cabbies here, so it helps to carry a map or the phone number of your destination in case you hail a driver who's new to the city and hasn't got his bearings yet.

Walking

Most cities in the UAE are very car-oriented and not designed to encourage walking. Additionally, summer temperatures of more than 45°C are not conducive to a leisurely stroll. The winter months, however, make walking quite pleasant. There aren't many pavements however, so you're best heading to places such as 2nd December Street, Dubai Creek and Jumeira Road for a wander. In late 2014, the Dhs.100 million 14 kilometre Jumeirah Corniche, running from Dubai Marine Resort

Street Strife

To make navigation more confusing, places may not always be referred to by their official name. For example, Jumeira Road is often known as Beach Road, and Interchange 1 on Sheikh Zayed Road is often called Defence Roundabout.

(dxbmarine.com) to the Burj Al Arab, opened fully and includes designated running paths, scenic walkways, retail kiosks and toilets. Bucking the current trend, Burj Khalifa and Marsa Dubai are attractive communities designed with pedestrians in mind. Both are interesting places to walk around with plenty of cafes and shops to tempt you off the street.

Water Bus

Crossing the creek by a traditional abra is a common method of transport for many people living in Bur Dubai and Deira; for visitors, it's a must-do experience while in town. Abra stations have been upgraded recently, but the fares are still just Dhs.1.

Another fun addition to the creek is a fleet of air-conditioned water buses. These operate on two different routes crossing the creek, with fares set at Dhs.2 per one way trip.

It's also possible to take a scenic cruise on RTA's new Dubai Ferry; the modern ferries whisk you on a scenic ride and the routes depart from Marsa Dubai and Al Ghubaiba. To keep up-to-date on all boating options on the creek, see rta.ae.

Further Out

If you want to explore the UAE during your stay then you'll need a driver or rental car. The east coast is known for its wonderful coastline and watersports, all within a two-hour drive. There is also a bus service to Abu Dhabi which runs hourly from Al Ghubaiba and Ibn Battuta bus stations. The journey takes two hours and costs Dhs.25. Contact the RTA on 800 9090 for more info.

Places To Stay

Nowhere does five-star like Dubai, but while there's a vast array of luxury options to choose from, there's also something to suit every budget.

In addition to a high number of plush hotels, Dubai has plenty of four, three, two and one-star places, self-catering villas, hotel apartments and even a youth hostel. Furthermore, a new hotel seems to spring up every few months, so you're never short of choice when it comes to deciding where to rest your head.

Most hotels are within 30 minutes of the airport and tend to be either on the beach, by the creek or on Sheikh Zayed Road. The coastal options will probably allow access to a private beach, but if you're in Dubai on business then proximity to the financial and business areas of DIFC and Trade Center is likely to be a priority. If you are in town to shop then take your pick as malls are everywhere – some with their own hotel. If you're here for a few days, why not combine your city stay with a night at a desert resort, such as Bab Al Shams?

Popular hotels tend to get fully booked up in the winter high season, but big discounts and attractive packages are offered to summer visitors when temperatures in Dubai soar.

The VIP Set

With Roberto Cavalli's Cavalli Club (cavalliclub. com) at the Fairmont and an Armani Hotel at Burj Khalifa (armanihotels.com), there are plenty of places to show off your designer threads.

The Address Downtown Dubai

theaddress.com
04 436 8888
This luxury hotel has a range of excellent restaurants and one of the coolest bars in the city, Neos. It has two sister hotels at The Dubai Mall (04 438 8888) and Dubai Marina (04 436 7777).
Map 2 B3 **Metro** Burj Khalifa/Dubai Mall

Image Courtesy of Emaar Properties

Armani Dubai

dubai.armanihotels.com
04 888 3888
Oozing style and extravagance, the Armani Hotel occupies six floors of the Burj Khalifa and has 160 exquisite rooms and suites. There are four restaurants, an opulent bar and a chic spa.
Map 2 B2 **Metro** Burj Khalifa/Dubai Mall

Ascott Park Place Dubai

the-ascott.com
04 310 8555
Located along the bustling Sheikh Zayed Road, Ascott's luxuriously kitted serviced apartments of various sizes are available for short or longer stays. The facilities include a 40m swimming pool and a gym.
Map 2 E1 **Metro** World Trade Centre

Atlantis, The Palm

atlantisthepalm.com
04 426 0000
Situated on the crescent of the Palm Jumeirah, the sugary pink Atlantis offers 1,539 rooms including The Lost Chambers Suites which feature floor-to-ceiling windows looking into the aquarium.
Map 1 C1 **Metro** Nakheel

Burj Al Arab

jumeirah.com
04 301 7777
Architecturally unique, one of the world's tallest hotels stands 321m high on a man-made island, and is dramatic, lavish and exclusive. Guests are looked after by a host of butlers. Reservations are essential for dining.
Map 3 E1 **Metro** Mall of the Emirates

Dubai Festival City

ihg.com
DFC has two hotels to choose from. The InterContinental (04 701 1111) has extensive spa facilities and great views from all of its rooms and suites; next door is the five-star Crowne Plaza (04 701 2222) with the popular Belgian Beer Cafe.
Map 1 J4 **Metro** Emirates

Hawthorn Suites
by Wyndham > *p.65*
hawthornsuitesdubai.com
04 399 9979
This accommodation has a variety of family entertainment and leisure activities. It features spacious suites with sea and marina view, and provides personalised hospitality.
Map 1 J5 **Metro** Jumeirah Lake Towers

Hilton Dubai Jumeirah Resort
hilton.com
04 399 1111
Situated on a private stretch of sand a stone's throw from The Walk, this resort boasts good watersports facilities and popular eateries such as BiCE and The Wavebreaker beach bar.
Map 3 A1 **Metro** Jumeirah Lakes Towers

Jumeirah Beach Hotel
jumeirah.com
04 348 0000
One of Dubai's major icons, this hotel is built in the shape of a wave with a colourful interior, and all rooms have a sea view. Bars and restaurants include Villa Beach, 360° and a new branch of Jamie's Italian.
Map 3 E1 **Metro** Mall of the Emirates

Le Royal Meridien Beach Resort & Spa

leroyalmeridien-dubai.com
04 399 5555
Set in landscaped gardens, this resort has a lush pool area and private beach, as well as excellent leisure facilities and a decent selection of bars and restaurants.
Map 3 B1 **Metro** DAMAC

Madinat Jumeirah

jumeirah.com
04 366 8888
This resort has two hotels, Al Qasr and Mina A'Salam, with 940 luxurious rooms and suites, and exclusive summer houses, all linked by man-made waterways. Between the hotels is Souk Madinat Jumeirah.
Map 3 E1 **Metro** Mall of the Emirates

One&Only Royal Mirage

oneandonlyroyalmirage.com
04 399 9999
Blessed with an intimate atmosphere, this hotel features unparalleled service and dining, while a luxury spa treatment here is pure indulgence. Try Moroccan cuisine at Tagine, or enjoy late nights at Kasbar.
Map 3 C1 **Metro** Nakheel

The Palace Downtown Dubai
theaddress.com
04 428 7888
Situated close to Burj Khalifa, The Palace boasts 242 deluxe rooms. There's butler service for all rooms, and views of the world's tallest building. Its Asado steak restaurant is recommended.
Map 2 B3 **Metro** Burj Khalifa/Dubai Mall

Park Hyatt Dubai
dubai.park.hyatt.com
04 602 1234
Mediterranean and Moorish in style, the Park Hyatt has 225 rooms, each with a balcony or terrace with great views. It has a prime waterfront location next to Dubai Creek Golf & Yacht Club.
Map 4 D5 **Metro** GGICO

Ramada Downtown Dubai > p.73
ramadadowntowndubai.com
04 330 7330
Located at the heart of Downtown Dubai, the hotel offers luxurious suites with vibrant interiors, spectacular views of Burj Khalifa and Dubai Fountain, along with excellent dining, recreational and meeting facilities.
Map 2 F6 **Metro** Burj Khalifa

The Ritz-Carlton Dubai

ritzcarlton.com
04 399 4000
Set right on the JBR beach, The Ritz-Carlton may stand low in comparison to the Marina towers but it excels in terms of style and service. Afternoon tea in the lobby is a must.
Map 3 A1 **Metro** DAMAC

Sheraton Dubai Mall of the Emirates

sheratondubaimalloftheemirates.com
04 377 2000
Located right next to the MoE, this plush hotel is a dream spot for keen shoppers. Also worth a mention is the roof terrace, which offers some of the best views in town.
Map 3 E2 **Metro** Mall of the Emirates

The Westin Dubai Mina Seyahi Beach Resort & Marina

westinminaseyahi.com
04 399 4141
The Westin offers all the luxury amenities you would expect of a five-star hotel – in addition to popular evening venues and 1,200m of private beach close to Marsa Dubai.
Map 3 B1 **Metro** Nakheel

Other Hotels

Burj Khalifa

With easy access to Dubai's financial centre and tourist attractions such as The Dubai Mall and Burj Khalifa, the Sheikh Zayed Road and Burj Khalifa hotels offer a balance of work and play. The glamorous Fairmont Dubai (04 332 5555, fairmont.com) sits opposite the city's financial hub and is home to some excellent dining options as well as Roberto Cavalli's signature nightspot, Cavalli Club. Nearby, the deluxe Shangri-La (04 343 8888, shangri-la.com) has a lovely pool area, as well as several popular bars and restaurants, including concept club The Act Dubai, which stylishly combines theatre, dining and nightlife. Located in the heart of Dubai's business district, the Ritz-Carlton Dubai International Financial Centre (04 372 2222, ritzcarlton.com) is a good bet for business trips; it's just steps away from DIFC and has good restaurants and a classy spa. Also in the DIFC area is Jumeirah Emirates Towers (04 330 0000, jumeirah.com), one of Dubai's most established luxury hotels. The nearby Dusit Thani (04 343 3333, dusit.com) lives up to its Thai ownership, housing the excellent far-eastern restaurant Benjarong.

Ski Stays

For the ultimate Dubai experience, check into Kempinski Hotel Mall of The Emirates (kempinski.com); located in the world's busiest mall, the hotel's exclusive chalet rooms boast views of the snowy slopes of Ski Dubai.

Marsa Dubai

With sea views, swimming pools and private beaches, sun worshippers are spoilt for choice in Marsa Dubai (formerly Dubai Marina) and JBR. The Habtoor Grand Beach Resort & Spa (04 399 5000, habtoorhotels.com) is another good option right on the beach. The Address Dubai Marina (04 436 7777, theaddress.com), meanwhile, boasts easy access to Dubai Marina Mall. The Dubai Marriott Harbour Hotel & Suites (04 319 4000, marriott.com) has spacious suites, each with its own kitchen and well-stocked bathroom. Nuran Marina Serviced Residences (04 367 4848, nuran.com) is also a good choice if apartment hotel convenience in the vicinity of the beach is what you're after; the well-equipped apartments boast stunning marina views and the complex is conveniently located between Dubai Marina Yacht Club (dubaimarinayachtclub.com) and Dubai Marina Mall.

The Palm

Other luxurious resorts to now join Atlantis on The Palm Jumeirah include Jumeirah Zabeel Saray (04 453 0000, jumeirah.com), One&Only The Palm (04 440 1010, oneandonlyresorts.com), and Anantara Dubai (04 567 8888, dubai-palm.anantara.com).

On The Creek

The creekside hotels are ideally located for soaking up the atmosphere of old Dubai. Jumeirah Creekside Hotel's unique, luxury interior will wow art lovers, and its Akaru Spa boasts plenty of awards. The **Sheraton Dubai Creek Hotel & Towers**

(04 228 1111, sheratondubaicreek.com) recent renovations mean upgraded comfort and services, and some stunning views. The Hilton Dubai Creek (04 227 1111, hilton.com) has some great restaurants, including Glasshouse Brasserie. Five-star Radisson Blu Hotel, Dubai Deira Creek (04 222 7171, radissonblu.com) has a scenic pool and a host of popular dining options; Fish Market is particularly recommended.

Near The Airport

Le Meridien Dubai (04 217 0000, lemeridien-dubai.com) offers easy access to the airport and the resort is home to some of the city's favourite restaurants, including the Meridien Village Terrace and Yalumba. The Al Bustan Rotana (04 282 0000, rotana.com) is another alternative in and around this residential neighbourhood.

Guesthouses & Hostels

Guesthouses in Dubai are few and far between, but the XVA Art Hotel (xvahotel.com) is a real hidden gem, nestled in a unique location in the heart of Al Fahidi Historical Neighbourhood, one of the oldest heritage sites in the region. XVA Art Hotel's seven guestrooms ooze rustic charm and the adjacent gallery hosts interesting art exhibitions.

Dubai Youth Hostel (04 298 8151, uaeyha.com) in the Al Qusais area, offers single, double, triple and dorm rooms starting from Dhs.100.

Villas are another option for short or longer stays; visit mydubaistay.com for accommodation in different areas, with online availability, booking and a cost comparison chart.

Out of the City

Al Maha Desert Resort & Spa

04 832 9900

Dubai-Al Ain Rd, Remah

al-maha.com

Set in 225 sq km of desert, the Al Maha resort, accessible only by a 4WD vehicle driven by your own field guide, is congruously set on the slopes of a rising dune and styled as a Bedouin camp. Wild Arabian oryx (*maha*) wander around the resort, and each guestroom is a stand-alone property, designed to resemble a traditional Bedouin tent. The suites feature a private terrace and infinity plunge pool. You can opt to dine in private on your patio or at the Al Diwaan restaurant; the choice is varied and there is a great wine list. The Saray Spa offers the full range of pampering and there are several activities you can take part in: one of the most popular is a sunset camel ride and champagne toast on the dunes.
Map 1 G7

Bab Al Shams Desert Resort & Spa

04 809 6100

Jebel Ali - Lehbab Rd, Mugatrah

meydanhotels.com

Like a desert mirage come to life, Bab Al Shams is a Bedouin fantasy escape. On approach, bamboo torches guide you to the low-rise building that blends into the imposing dunes that surround it, and the rooms have been designed to evoke a feeling of Bedouin living. Camel rides on the sand dunes are offered to guests, or you can chill out in one of the outdoor holistic swimming pools. Take the pampering up a notch by heading to the Satori Spa and, as the evening sets in, Al Sarab Rooftop Lounge offers shisha and drinks. The Al Hadheerah restaurant offers a full-on Arabian experience, including a huge buffet, belly dancing and traditional music. **Map** 1 D7

JA Jebel Ali Golf Resort

04 814 5555

Nr Palm Jebel Ali, Jabal Ali   jaresortshotels.com

Just far enough out of Dubai to escape the hustle and bustle, this resort offers luxurious stays in resplendent surroundings, with a peaceful atmosphere. Set within 128 acres of lush, landscaped gardens, the recently renovated resort boasts an 800m private beach, a marina and a golf course. Guests can also enjoy horse riding, shooting, tennis, mini-golf and a variety of watersports. **Map** 1 A2

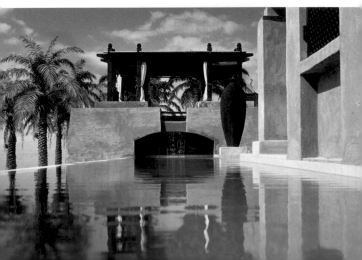

Exploring

Explore Dubai	80
Al Fahidi Historical Neighbourhood	84
Deira & The Creek: Dubai's Port	90
Downtown & Sheikh Zayed Road	96
Marsa Dubai & JBR: New Dubai	102
Festival City & Garhoud	106
Jumeira: Beachside Life	110
Palm Jumeirah & Al Sufouh	116
Umm Hurair: Creekside Adventure	122
Off The Beaten Track	126
Further Out	130
Tours & Sightseeing	140

Explore Dubai

From slick city attractions to expansive deserts, Dubai is an emirate of superlatives that will impress even the most seasoned traveller.

Dubai provides a wealth of contrasting images: Ferraris parked outside falafel shops, massive skyscrapers shading pristine mosques, billionaires, cranes, camels, palaces and windtowers. The city is filled with luxurious five-star hotels and huge shopping malls, it has some of the top nightspots in the Middle East, and is home to a range of museums, heritage sites and places of cultural interest. Quite a mix.

Don't let the traffic and ever-expanding footprint disorientate you – Dubai itself is fairly easy to navigate and explore, especially with the introduction of the metro. The city runs along the Arabian Gulf coast, and the older and more bustling sections of the city, such as Deira and Bur Dubai, are situated in the northern end and around Dubai Creek. From there, the city stretches south along Sheikh Zayed Road towards developments such as The Palm and Marsa Dubai.

Most of the city's historical attractions are located around the creek which, until recently, was the residential and commercial hub of the city. Al Fahidi Historical Neighbourhood and the souks of Deira have managed to retain much of the old Dubai character and multiculturalism, with narrow streets selling everything from wholesale grain

The bright lights of Deira

to traditional Emirati dress. These are also the best areas to find a traditional Indian or Arabic meal. Try Saravana Bhavan for a spicy south-Indian thali, or Bastakiah Nights for a taste of Emirati *machboos*. If large and luxurious better describes the Dubai of your dreams, newer areas like Downtown Dubai, home to the world's tallest building, and Marsa Dubai should be your target destinations. The towering skyscrapers and enormous malls that fill these impressive developments contain some of the best shopping and nightlife in the Middle East. The Dubai Mall houses some 1,200 shops, while the sheer volume of restaurants and bars on the Al Sufouh strip, The Palm and the marina could easily keep you occupied for years.

Heritage Sites

Al Ahmadiya School & Heritage House   p.92
Heritage & Diving Villages   p.85
Iranian Mosque   p.127
Jumeirah Mosque   p.111
Majlis Ghorfat Um Al Sheef   p.112
Sheikh Mohammed Centre For
  Cultural Understanding   p.86
Sheikh Saeed Al Maktoum's House   p.86

Museums & Art Galleries

Dubai International Art Centre   p.111
Dubai Museum   p.85
Gallery Isabelle van den Eynde   p.126
Opera Gallery   p.128
The jamjar   p.127
The Majlis Gallery   p.86
The Third Line   p.129
XVA Gallery   p.87

Parks

Creek Park   p.122
Safa Park   p.113
Zabeel Park   p.123

Beaches & Beach Parks

Jumeirah Open Beach p.112
Mamzar Beach Park p.92
Jumeirah Beach Park p.111

Amusement & Water Parks

Children's City p.122
SEGA Republic p.99
Wild Wadi Water Park p.118

Sights & Attractions

Atlantis, The Palm p.117
Burj Al Arab p.117
Creekside Souks p.93
Dubai Aquarium & Underwater Zoo p.97
Dubai Dolphinarium p.93
The Dubai Fountain p.98
Global Village p.126
Jumeirah Emirates Towers p.98
Karama p.128
Marina Walk p.103
Plant Street p.128
Souk Madinat Jumeirah p.118
The Beach at Jumeirah Beach Residence p.103

Exploring

At A Glance

Al Fahidi Historical Neighbourhood

For a glimpse into Dubai's past, Al Fahidi Historical Neighbourhood and Al Shindagha's narrow streets are not to be missed.

If you're in search of a dose of tradition, step into a pocket of the city that harks back to a bygone era. Al Fahidi Historical Neighbourhood (previously known as Bastakiya) and Al Shindagha are some of the oldest heritage sites in Dubai and certainly the most atmospheric. The neighbourhood dates from the early 1900s when traders from the Bastakiya area of southern Iran were encouraged to settle there by tax concessions granted by Sheikh Maktoum bin Hashar, the ruler of Dubai at the time.

The area is characterised by traditional windtower houses, built around courtyards and clustered together along winding alleyways. The distinctive four-sided windtowers (*barjeel*), seen on top of the traditional flat-roofed buildings, were an early form of air conditioning.

There are some excellent cultural establishments in and around Al Fahidi Historical Neighbourhood and Al Shindagha, and a short stroll along the creek will bring you to the Textile Souk and abra station, from where you can cross the water to explore the souks on the Deira side. You can make a single crossing on a communal abra for Dhs.1, or hire your own (plus driver) for an hour-long tour for Dhs.100, or take a water bus.

Dubai Museum

04 353 1862

Al Fahidi St, Al Souk Al Kabeer   dubaiculture.ae

Located in and under Al Fahidi Fort, which dates back to 1787, this museum is creative and well thought-out. All parts of life from Dubai's past are represented in an attractive and interesting way; walk through a souk from the 1950s, stroll through an oasis, see into a traditional house, get up close to local wildlife, learn about the archaeological finds or go 'underwater' to discover the pearl diving and fishing industries. There are some entertaining mannequins to pose with too. Entry costs Dhs.3 for adults and Dhs.1 for children under six years old. Open daily 8.30am to 8.30pm (2pm to 5pm on Fridays). **Map** 4 C2 **Metro** Al Fahidi

Heritage & Diving Villages

04 393 7151

Al Khaleej St,
  Al Shindagha   dubaiculture.ae

Located near the mouth of Dubai Creek, the Heritage & Diving Villages focus on Dubai's maritime past, pearl diving traditions and architecture. Visitors can observe traditional potters and weavers practising their craft the way it has been done for centuries. Local women serve traditionally cooked snacks – one of the rare opportunities you'll have to sample genuine Emirati cuisine. Camel rides are also available most afternoons and evenings. The Village is particularly lively during the Dubai Shopping Festival and Eid celebrations, with performances including traditional sword dancing. Open daily 8.30am to 10pm (Fridays 3.30pm to 10pm). **Map** 4 C1 **Metro** Al Ghubaiba

The Majlis Gallery
04 353 6233

Al Fahidi Historical Neighbourhood,
Al Souk Al Kabeer
themajlisgallery.com

The Majlis Gallery is a converted Arabian house, complete
with windtowers and courtyard. Small, whitewashed
rooms lead off the central garden and host exhibitions by
contemporary artists. In addition to the fine art collection,
there's an extensive range of hand-made glass, pottery,
fabrics, frames and unusual furniture. Open Saturday to
Thursday, 10am to 6pm. **Map** 4 C2 **Metro** Al Fahidi

Sheikh Mohammed Centre
for Cultural Understanding
04 353 6666

Al Fahidi Historical Neighbourhood,
Al Souk Al Kabeer
cultures.ae

This facility helps visitors and residents understand the
customs and traditions of the UAE. It organises guided tours
in Jumeirah Mosque, a walking tour of the Al Souk Al Kabeer
area, as well as cultural breakfasts and lunches. There are
majlis-style rooms around the courtyard and great views.
Open Sunday to Thursday 8am to 6pm and Saturday 9am to
1pm. **Map** 4 C2 **Metro** Al Fahidi

Sheikh Saeed Al Maktoum House
04 393 7139

Al Khaleej St,
Al Shindagha
dubaiculture.ae

Dating from 1896, this carefully restored house-turned-
museum is built in the traditional manner of the Gulf coast,
using coral covered in lime and sand-coloured plaster. The

Heritage & Diving Villages

interesting displays in many rooms show rare and wonderful photographs of life in Dubai pre-oil – totally different from today. Entry is Dhs.2 for adults, Dhs.1 for children.
Map 4 C1 **Metro** Al Ghubaiba

XVA Gallery

04 353 5383

Al Fahidi Historical Neighbourhood,
Al Souk Al Kabeer

xvagallery.com

This is one of Dubai's most interesting art galleries. Originally a windtower house, it's worth a visit for its architecture alone, which has a true authentic look and feel. The gallery hosts exhibitions throughout the year and there's also a boutique hotel with guestrooms. Open daily.
Map 4 C2 **Metro** Al Fahidi

If you only do one thing in...
Old Dubai

Get schooled at the informative Dubai Museum.
Learn about life in Dubai 50 years ago.

Best for...

Eating & Drinking: For an atmospheric evening of
Arabian food in a traditional setting, book a table at
Bastakiah Nights.

Families: Let the kids hop on a camel while you gorge
on freshly baked bread, all in the middle of living history
at the Heritage & Diving Villages.

Relaxation: Duck into tranquillity at The Majlis Gallery
or XVA.

Shopping: A visit to the Textile Souk is a memorable
affair, and if your haggling skills are up to par you could
take home a pashmina at a bargain price.

Sightseeing: The winding alleyways of Al Fahidi
Historical Neighbourhood will linger in the memory long
after you leave Dubai.

Traditional Arabian architecture

Al Fahidi Historical Neighbourhood

Deira & The Creek: Dubai's Port

Deira's busy streets capture the bustling essence of old Dubai, while the emirate's trading traditions live on at the creek.

Once the residential hub of Dubai, Deira remains an incredibly atmospheric area. Narrow convoluted streets bustle with activity, while gold, spices, perfumes and general goods are touted in its numerous souks. Likewise, Dubai Creek, upon which Deira sits, was once the centre of Dubai commerce. Both sides of the creek are lined by corniches that come alive in the evenings as residents head out for a stroll and traders take stock. Take the time to meander along the Deira side of the creek where men in traditional south-Asian garb unload wooden dhows that are docked by the water's edge and tightly packed with everything from fruit and vegetables to televisions and maybe even a car or two. And no visitor should leave without experiencing a trip across the water on a commuter abra for Dhs.1, or a tourist abra (Dhs.100 for an hour's private trip).

Start with a wander through the Textile Souk on the Bur Dubai side, before taking an abra towards Deira. Once on the Deira side, cross the corniche and head towards the souk district. First stop is the Spice Souk (where the aroma of saffron and cumin fills the air. Nearby, the streets in and around the Gold Souk are filled with shops shimmering with gold and platinum. If it's exotic rugs you're after, then Deira Tower on Al Nasr Square (Map 4 D2) is worth a visit. Around 40 shops offer a colourful profusion of carpets from Iran,

Clocktower Roundabout

Pakistan, Turkey and Afghanistan, to suit everyone's taste and pocket. For dinner with a view, head to the top of the Hyatt Regency where Al Dawaar hosts an incredible buffet within its rotating dining room. Afterwards, go for a stroll along the Gulf side of Deira corniche. If you're staying on the Deira side of town, Al Mamzar has a great section of beach (see below).

Al Ahmadiya School & Heritage House

04 226 0286
Al Ahmadiya St, Al Ras   dubaiculture.ae
Established in 1912 for Dubai's elite, Al Ahmadiya School was the earliest regular school in the city. A visit here is an excellent opportunity to see the history of education in the UAE. Situated in what is becoming a small centre for heritage (Al Souk Al Kabeer), it is an interesting example of a traditional Emirati family home, and dates back to 1890. Admission to both is free. Open Saturday to Thursday 8.30am to 8.30pm and 2pm to 8.30pm on Friday. **Map** 4 C1 **Metro** Al Ras

Mamzar Beach Park

04 296 6201
Al Khaleej St, Al Mamzar   dm.gov.ae
With its four clean beaches, open spaces and plenty of greenery, Al Mamzar is a popular spot. The well-maintained beaches have sheltered areas for swimming and changing rooms with showers. Air-conditioned chalets, with barbecues, can be rented on a daily basis, costing from Dhs.160 to Dhs.210. There are two swimming pools with lifeguards on duty. Entrance is Dhs.5 per person or Dhs.30 per car (including all occupants). **Map** 1 K2 **Metro** Al Qiyadah

Creekside Souks

Al Ras

Deira's three main souks – the Spice Souk, the Fish Souk and the Gold Souk – present some of the best examples of living heritage that Dubai has to offer. Smelly as it may be, an early morning trip through the Fish Souk makes for a great photo opportunity. The Gold Souk gets crowded on weekend afternoons, but spend an hour or two here during the week and enjoy a form of window shopping that's very different from a mall experience. For the best insight into the region's varied cuisines, take a walk through the Spice Souk where you'll be bombarded by the colours and smells of spices you've never heard of. Just across the creek on the Bur Dubai side sits the covered Textile Souk with its myriad of bright fabrics. An abra ride across the creek is a must while in this part of town. **Map** 4 C2 **Metro** Al Ras

Dubai Dolphinarium > *p.vi, vii* 04 336 9773

Gate 1, Creek Park, Umm Hurair 2   dubaidolphinarium.ae

Located within Creek Park, the main attraction here is the seal and dolphin show, which runs twice a day during the week and three times daily at the weekends (closed on Sundays). Afterwards, you can get your picture taken with the friendly mammals. Prices start at Dhs.100 for adults and Dhs.50 for children; check the website for details of other options, including a chance to swim with the dolphins. Don't miss the mirror maze and the daily exotic bird show, which features performing parrots, cockatoos and macaws – the only show of its kind in the UAE. **Map** 4 C5 **Metro** Dubai Healthcare City

If you only do one thing in...
Deira & The Creek

Watch the dhows unload at the corniche, then head for a stroll around Dubai's famous souks.

Best for...

Eating & Drinking: Hop on a dhow for a delicious dinner cruise. This is by far the best way to get your fill of food, facts and photographs.

Families: Give the kids an experience of a lifetime at the Dubai Dolphinarium.

Relaxation: Step into the calm courtyard of the Al Ahmadiya School & Heritage House, where you'll find some quiet in the Deira storm.

Shopping: Stroll through the glittering streets of the Gold Souk before following your nose to the Spice Souk.

Sightseeing: Reserve a table at the Hyatt Regency's Al Dawaar. The city's only revolving restaurant offers fantastic views of the creek and beyond.

Clockwise from top: an abra on Dubai Creek, Spice Souk, a dhow close-up

Downtown & Sheikh Zayed Road

The world's tallest building, Dubai's largest mall and the most photographed skyline in the city are all in Dubai's glitziest area.

Among the newest places in town to explore, Downtown Dubai is a spectacular mix of shops, restaurants, entertainment and architecture, while nearby is a stretch of Dubai's original stunning skyscraper strip, which lines either side of Sheikh Zayed Road and features some of the city's top hotels and building designs. At the heart of Downtown Dubai is the shimmering Burj Khalifa; the world's tallest tower points like a needle more than 800m skywards and counts an Armani hotel, viewing platforms At The Top and At The Top, Burj Khalifa SKY and the world's highest restaurant, At. mosphere, among its attractions. By its base are The Dubai Mall, Old Town, and The Dubai Fountain.

The Dubai Mall is a huge shopping centre full of top-end retail brands, excellent eateries and some fantastic entertainment options, such as Dubai Aquarium and SEGA Republic. There are two The Address hotels in the area, with the views from the 63rd floor Neos bar at The Address Downtown Dubai well worth taking in. Old Town, which is home to the atmospheric Souk Al Bahar, takes strong influences from traditional Arabia with its mosaics, passageways and fortress-like finishes, all of which are beautifully lit at night. Other hotels in the Downtown area include The Palace and Al Manzil, which are home to Asado steakhouse and upmarket sports bar Nezesaussi respectively.

The buzzing strip over on Sheikh Zayed Road is known for the striking architecture of its high-rise residential buildings, office towers and top-class hotels. From the Dubai World Trade Centre to Interchange 1 (known as Defence Roundabout), the wide, skyscraping 3.5km stretch is the subject of many a photo, as well as after-hours hook-ups in the various happening hotspots. With so many residents, tourists and business people around, this area really comes alive at night, as the crowds flit from restaurants to bars to clubs in the area's many hotels.

Dubai Aquarium & Underwater Zoo > p.203

04 448 5200

The Dubai Mall, Downtown Dubai, Burj Khalifa

thedubaiaquarium.com

More than 33,000 tropical fish are displayed to passing shoppers free of charge in a huge fish tank. For a closer view of the main tank's inhabitants, which include fearsome looking sand tiger sharks, you can pay to walk through the 270° viewing tunnel. Also well worth a look is the Underwater Zoo, which has residents such as penguins, piranhas and an octopus. The newest resident is a giant crocodile called King Croc. He weighs 750kgs and is more than 5m in length. If you're feeling adventurous, you can even go for a scuba dive in the tank (call ahead to book). A ticket to the interactive Underwater Zoo and Tunnel Experience costs Dhs.70 for adults and Dhs.55 for children. **Map** 2 C3 **Metro** Burj Khalifa/Dubai Mall

The Dubai Fountain

800 382 246 255

Nr Burj Khalifa,
  Downtown Dubai, Burj Khalifa   thedubaimall.com

This spectacular Downtown centrepiece draws crowds to witness the regular evening shows. Designed by the same team that created the famous Bellagio fountains in Las Vegas, the water, light and music combination is a captivating showstopper. Jets of water shoot 150m into the air along the length of the Burj lake in synchronisation with classical and Arabic music, while the Burj Khalifa at night forms a memorable backdrop. The show takes place daily at 1pm and 1.30pm, and then every half hour from 6pm until 11pm (weekdays) or 11.30pm (weekends). It can be viewed from outside The Dubai Mall and Souk Al Bahar, or you could grab a table at one of the many outdoor restaurants in this area.
Map 2 C3 **Metro** Burj Khalifa/Dubai Mall

Jumeirah Emirates Towers

04 330 0000

Sheikh Zayed Rd, Trade Center 2   jumeirah.com

These twin towers are a true Dubai landmark. At 350m, the office tower was the tallest building in the Middle East and Europe until the Burj Khalifa surpassed it. The smaller tower, at 305m, houses the Emirates Towers Hotel plus many eating and drinking spots. Harry Ghatto's is a city favourite for karaoke, while the Ivy (04 319 8767) offers fine fare. For a scenic thrill, the views from the aptly named 51st floor Alta Badia Bar are superb. If shopping makes your heart beat, The Boulevard is probably Dubai's most exclusive mall.
Map 2 D2 **Metro** Emirates Towers

The Dubai Fountain & Old Town Island

SEGA Republic > *p.IFC*

The Dubai Mall,
 Downtown Dubai, Burj Khalifa

04 448 8484

segarepublic.com

This indoor theme park located in The Dubai Mall offers a range of indoor thrills, courtesy of the nine main attractions and the 200 arcade games. A Power Pass (Dhs.175) gets you all-day access to the big attractions, which include stomach-flipping rides like the Sonic Hopper, the SpinGear and the Halfpipe Canyon. Unlike many other shopping mall amusement centres, SEGA Republic is for all ages, and features some truly unique thrills.
Map 2 C3 **Metro** Burj Khalifa/Dubai Mall

If you only do one thing in...
Downtown Dubai & Sheikh Zayed Road

Dine alfresco while watching the nightly Dubai Fountain shows.

Best for...

Eating & Drinking: Japanese restaurant Zuma in DIFC offers one of the best, funkiest, fine-dining experiences in Dubai.

Families: Take the kids to SEGA Republic and be amazed at how far technology has come.

Relaxation: Take time out at The Spa at The Palace; after a treatment here you'll feel like royalty (04 428 7805).

Shopping: With over 1,000 stores, The Dubai Mall is a shopaholic's paradise.

Sightseeing: The sweeping views from the world's highest restaurant At.mosphere can't be beaten.

Clockwise from top: Old Town, Emirates Towers, The Dubai Aquarium

Downtown & Sheikh Zayed Road

Marsa Dubai & JBR: New Dubai

Head to Marsa Dubai for high-rise heaven, a thriving cafe culture and bustling beach action.

Previously home to just a handful of waterfront hotels, Marsa Dubai (formerly Dubai Marina) is the epitome of the rise of 'New Dubai' to modern prominence. Apartment buildings (finished or still under construction) have sprouted up along every inch of the man-made waterway, while between the inland marina and the shore is the massive Jumeirah Beach Residence (JBR) development, which now dwarfs the five-star beach resorts such as the Hilton and Ritz-Carlton. The walkways that run around the marina and parallel to the coast have evolved into lively strips of cafes and restaurants, which throng with people in the evenings when the lit-up skyscrapers are at their most impressive. On the water, luxury boats fill the marina's berths, and thrill seekers take to the sea to parasail or waterski.

JBR Beach
Marsa Dubai
At nearly 2km long, this bay of golden sand is very popular. The space in front of hotels is reserved for guests, but there are plenty of areas in between for others. The sea is calm and good for swimming, and hotels offer a variety of watersports such as parasailing that anyone can sign up for. The outdoor shopping and dining development The Beach has just opened, whilst several hotel extensions and the world's largest Ferris wheel are still under construction. **Map** 3 A1 **Metro** DAMAC

The Beach at Jumeirah Beach Residence

Jumeirah Beach Residence, Marsa Dubai   04 431 0190

Shopping and dining destination The Beach has just opened its doors under the shadow of Jumeirah Beach Residence, boasting a 30,000 square foot, beachside location. A host of alfresco dining options are located on the beach promenade, whilst shops and further dining options occupy the low-rise open-air mall just behind it. A large car park provides 1,200 spaces and costs Dhs.20 per hour unless you meet the minimum spend of Dhs.75 in cafes and restaurants.

Movie fans can get their fix at the 10 screen multiplex cinema or enjoy a movie alfresco at the UAE's first outdoor cinema.

Jumeirah Beach Residence's original outdoor dining and shopping destination The Walk is located just behind the development. **Map** 3 A1 **Metro** DAMAC

Marina Walk

Marsa Dubai

Marina Walk boulevard starts at the base of Dubai Marina Towers and provides an almost continuous pedestrian access around the 11km perimeter of the water. The area comes to life in the evenings and cooler months, when you can enjoy a meal in one of the waterfront restaurants and gaze out across the rows of yachts and the flashing lights of high-rise hotels and apartments. For speedier explorations, you'll find bicycle rental spots along the way. Dubai Marina Mall, and Dubai Marina Yacht Club are also located on the walk.
Map 3 A1 **Metro** DAMAC

Exploring

If you only do one thing in...
Marsa Dubai & JBR

Head to the beach for a morning swim before treating yourself to an alfresco breakfast on The Walk.

Best for...

Eating & Drinking: Tuck into seafood alfresco at Dubai Marina Yacht Club's Aquara and watch marina life sail by as you dine.

Families: Give the family the thrill of a lifetime with a camel ride on JBR Beach.

Relaxation: End your day on the beach by taking a leisurely stroll along the golden sands, then head out to Ritz-Carlton's opulent spa for a spot of pampering.

Shopping: Step off the beach and into alfresco mall The Beach, where you can happily browse a choice of fashion, beauty, and kidswear.

Sightseeing: Take the hour-long Captain Jack dhow tour (Bristol Middle East) for some spectacular views of the marina and JBR from the water.

Waterside living in Marsa Dubai

Marsa Dubai & JBR: New Dubai

Festival City & Garhoud

Relaxed and refined, Festival City is an oasis of calm in an otherwise rushed, modern metropolis.

Situated on the creek just down from Deira, Festival City has grown into a massive eating, shopping and entertainment complex. With an open marina, a bowling centre and cinema, a world-class golf course and several restaurants, Festival City has enough attractions to warrant a day of exploring, strolling and window shopping.

Festival City is bounded at one end by Al Badia Golf Club and its gorgeous clubhouse, and at the other by the InterContinental and Crowne Plaza hotel towers which house the Belgian Beer Cafe. In between sits the Festival Waterfront Centre, one of Dubai's more spacious and relaxed shopping malls, as well as an outdoor concert venue that has hosted Paul Weller, Kylie Minogue, Maroon 5 and Queen. A canal-like waterway, complete with tiny passenger boats and alfresco dining options, meanders through the area and is perfect for post-meal, evening strolls. For a truly authentic dining experience, look no further than Al Fanar, an atmospheric restaurant that specialises in Emirati cuisine. Aside from shopping and dining, Festival City hosts several events throughout the year, including dragonboat races, children's events and fashion shows. Check out festivalcentre.com for a schedule of upcoming events. Nearby in Garhoud, the Irish Village has long been an institution on the Dubai party scene

Dubai Festival City

with live music and several annual events such as the Dubai Sound City music festival. Next door, the Century Village is a collection of licensed alfresco restaurants including Sushi Sushi (04 282 9908) and St Tropez (04 286 9029). The Dubai Tennis Stadium is home of the Dubai Duty Free Tennis Championships, while The Aviation Club has good fitness and leisure facilities; a new hotel is also underway here. A bit closer to Deira is the Dubai Creek Golf & Yacht Club, incorporating the creekside Boardwalk restaurant and Park Hyatt Dubai, home to the lovely Amara Spa and The Thai Kitchen restaurant.

Festival City & Garhoud

If you only do one thing in...
Festival City & Garhoud

Spend an evening over pints and live music at the Irish Village, one of the city's oldest and most popular pubs.

Best for...

Eating & Drinking: Tuck into regional specialities at Emirati restaurant Al Fanar.

Families: The bowling alley in Festival Waterfront Centre is a blast for all ages.

Sightseeing: The views from Boardwalk are some of the best in the city.

Shopping: The spacious, well-designed halls of Festival Waterfront Centre offer a calmer shopping environment than the busier, larger malls.

Relaxation: Indulge yourself with a treatment at the highly rated Amara Spa at the Park Hyatt Dubai.

Jumeira: Beachside Life

Jumeira's beaches, boutiques and art galleries offer a pleasant retreat from the city's bustling core.

Jumeira might not have the exotic atmosphere or history of Deira, but its beaches, shopping centres and pleasant, wide roads make up for it. Head out here for a glimpse into the good life: Jumeira is one of the most desirable addresses for well-off expats and home to the infamous, coiffeured 'Jumeira Janes' – well-off expat women who can often be found in the boutiques along Jumeira Road and the shops in Mercato Mall.

The popular Jumeirah Open Beach is open to all free of charge, with a new 14 kilometre beachfront corniche offering a wide walkway, jogging track, retail kiosks, and public showes and toilets. Just outside Jumeira, on the border with Satwa, lies 2nd December Street – the main destination for anyone needing to feed their post-club hunger, show off their expensive customised cars, or watch the city pass by as they enjoy some street-side Lebanese fare. If you're out past midnight, don't miss having a bite at either Al Mallah or Ravi's Pakistani restaurant, which is cheap as chips and offers authentic and tasty dishes.

Don't think that Jumeira doesn't have culture; Jumeirah Mosque is one of the most recognisable places of worship in the city and welcomes tourists with tours, and the many galleries will keep art enthusiasts happy.

Dubai International Art Centre
04 344 4398

Villa 27, 75B St, Jumeira 1   artdubai.com

Since its founding in 1976, Dubai International Art Centre has been a hub for all things artsy in Jumeira. In addition to nurturing local talent by organising training and workshops, the premises also house Gallery 76. This exhibition venue has been hosting interesting displays of art by local and international artists alike since 2005; the exhibitions range from paintings, sculpture and photography to outdoor installations. **Map** 1 G2 **Metro** Business Bay

Jumeirah Beach Park
04 349 2555

Jumeira St, Jumeira 2   dm.gov.ae

Formerly a popular park with grassed picnic areas, a cafe and trees lining the beach, this park has been closed while the Dubai Canal is constructed. It will re-open in 2016, by which time, Dubai's new waterway will run through it and out into the sea. In the meantime, the best bet is to head to Jumeirah Open Beach (see next page), to the left of this beach (as you face the sea), as it boasts the same views and is free to access. **Map** 1 G2 **Metro** Business Bay

Jumeirah Mosque
04 353 6666

Jumeira St, Jumeira 1   cultures.ae

This is the most beautiful mosque in the city. Non-Muslims are not usually permitted entry to a mosque, but the Sheikh Mohammed Centre for Cultural Understanding organises weekly tours (Saturday, Sunday, Tuesday and Thursday mornings at 10am). Visitors are guided around the mosque

before receiving a talk on Islam and the prayer ritual. Dress conservatively – no shorts or sleeveless tops. Women must also cover their hair with a head scarf, and all visitors should remove their shoes. Cameras are allowed and large groups can book private mosque tours.
Map 1 H2 **Metro** World Trade Centre

Jumeirah Open Beach

Nr Dubai Marine Beach Resort & Spa, Jumeira 1
One of the most popular free beaches in the city, this clean area has been revamped with the opening of the 14 kilometre Jumeirah Corniche in late 2014. Starting near Dubai Marine Beach Resort & Spa, it features a wide walkway, jogging track, retail kiosks, and public showers and toilets, all overlooking the white sand and turquoise shore. Unfortunately, men staring at the sunbathing women can often be found loitering, but generally they mean no harm. At the start of 2015, the beach to the right of Jumeirah Beach Park (as you face the sea) was temporarily closed. **Map** 1 H2 **Metro** Emirates Towers

Majlis Ghorfat Um Al Sheif

04 852 1374
dubaiculture.ae

Al Mehemal St, Jumeira 3
Constructed in 1955 from coral stone and gypsum, this simple building was used by the late Sheikh Rashid bin Saeed Al Maktoum as a summer residence. The ground floor is an open veranda, while upstairs the *majlis* (meeting place) is decorated with carpets, cushions, lanterns and rifles. The Majlis is located just off Jumeira Road on Street 17, beside

Jumeirah Mosque

HSBC bank. Entry is Dhs.1 for adults and free for children under six years old. It opens at 8.30am and closes at 8.30pm every day except Friday, when it opens at 2.30pm.
Map 1 F2 **Metro** Business Bay

Safa Park

04 349 2111
Al Wasl St, Al Wasl
dm.gov.ae

A large and picturesque park where locals and expats come together. There's a boating lake, tennis and basketball courts, barbecue areas, and plenty of kids' play areas. Entry costs Dhs.3 (free for children under three years old). There's a great running track around the park's perimeter. However, the park is partially closed for the construction of Dubai Canal, which will eventually flow through it when it is completed in 2016.
Map 1 G2 **Metro** Business Bay

If you only do one thing in...
Jumeira

Take a tour of the most beautiful mosque in the city, and one of the few in the country open to non-Muslims.

Best for...

Eating & Drinking: Dine on fantastic Cuban fare while listening to a live Latino band at El Malecon.

Families: Spread out a towel on the sand of Jumeirah Open Beach, paddle in the sea, and experience the Dubai you've seen in the brochures.

Relaxation: Feel like a 'Jumeira Jane' by slipping into SensAsia Urban Spa for a treatment (04 349 8850).

Shopping: Enjoy a wander through the malls and independent fashion boutiques of Jumeira Road.

Sightseeing: Stroll Jumeirah Corniche late in the afternoon and glance back towards the city for a photo-worthy view as the sun sets.

Jumeira: Beachside Life

Palm Jumeirah & Al Sufouh

With a modern man-made wonder, world-famous hotels, sandy shores and an indoor ski slope, this area is a must for any itinerary.

This stretch of coastline, between Marsa Dubai and Umm Suqeim, is home to some of the most prestigious and popular resorts in Dubai. From the exclusive, iconic Burj Al Arab and Jumeirah Beach Hotel at one end, along Al Sufouh Road past the One&Only Royal Mirage, The Westin and, finally, at the other end, Le Meridien Mina Seyahi (with everyone's favourite beach party bar, Barasti), this section of the Gulf contains more pricey hotels than a Monopoly set. In the middle of all this, stretching several kilometres out to sea, is The Palm, Dubai's original mind-boggling man-made island, with its countless luxury villas and apartments, and the Disney-esque Atlantis hotel as its crowning showpiece. Within these resorts are dozens of excellent eating and drinking choices, open to all, while Souk Madinat Jumeirah and, nearby in Al Barsha, Mall of the Emirates are both great spots for shopping, dining and all-round entertainment.

Sun and water lovers are well catered for here too, with two water parks (Wild Wadi and Aquaventure), a great public beach and several full-service private hotel beaches available for day use. If the beautiful weather gets to be too much, there's always Ski Dubai where you can have a jaunt in the snow to cool you down.

Atlantis, The Palm

04 426 0000

Crescent St,
Palm Jumeirah, Nakhlat Jumeira   atlantisthepalm.com

As the name suggests, the water theme is an important part
of the Atlantis set-up. Aquaventure is the resort's thrilling
water park; get the adrenaline pumping by making the Leap
of Faith, a 27.5m near-vertical drop, or take the various slides
that shoot you through a series of tunnels surrounded by
shark-infested waters. Alternatively, The Rapids will carry you
around a 2.3km river, complete with waterfalls and wave
surges. Another attraction here is Dolphin Bay, where you can
get close up in the water with playful bottlenose dolphins,
while inside the hotel is the Lost Chambers Aquarium, which
contains 65,000 colourful inhabitants. The hotel is also home
to several top restaurants, including Nobu and La Brasserie
(formerly Rostang). **Map** 1 C1 **Metro** Nakheel

Burj Al Arab

04 301 7777

Jumeira St, Umm Suqeim 3   jumeirah.com

The Burj Al Arab is one of the most photographed sights
in Dubai. The billowing sail structure is a stunning piece
of architecture – and inside it's no less spectacular. If your
budget allows, you shouldn't miss the opportunity to sample
luxury at the spa, bars and restaurants; try the afternoon tea
at Sahn Eddar or the Skyview Bar, and fine seafood dining
at Al Mahara. Keep in mind that you won't be allowed into
the Burj Al Arab unless you have a reservation at one of the
dining venues. Advanced booking is required.
Map 3 E1 **Metro** Mall of the Emirates

Souk Madinat Jumeirah

Jumeira St, Al Sufouh 1

Souk Madinat Jumeirah is located just a stone's throw from the Burj Al Arab and next-door neighbour Al Qasr. Built to resemble a traditional Arabian market, the souk is a maze of alleyways featuring 95 open-fronted shops and boutiques where you can find everything from swimwear to souvenirs. There are numerous coffee shops and bars, as well as a theatre. For weary shoppers, there's Talise, an outstanding spa in the adjacent hotel. This is also a popular destination for dining, including Chinese fusion at Zheng He's at Mina A'Salam hotel. **Map** 3 E1 **Metro** Mall of the Emirates

Wild Wadi Water Park > *p.ix*

04 348 4444
wildwadi.com

Jumeira St, Umm Suqeim 3

Spread over 12 acres beside Jumeirah Beach Hotel, Wild Wadi caters for all ages and bravery levels. There can be queues, but the wait is worth it, and once you've paid to enter there is no limit to the number of times you can ride. The park is home to over 30 scream-inducing rides and attractions. It opens at 10am and the closing time depends on the time of year. Admission is Dhs.255 for adults and Dhs.195 for children. Thursday is ladies' night for those girls who'd rather not show their skin to everyone. There is also a 'sundowner' rate (for the last two hours of opening), check with Wild Wadi directly as prices are subject to change, children's entrance fees vary depending on their height. Check the website for up-to-date opening times.
Map 3 E1 **Metro** Mall of the Emirates

Palm Jumeirah

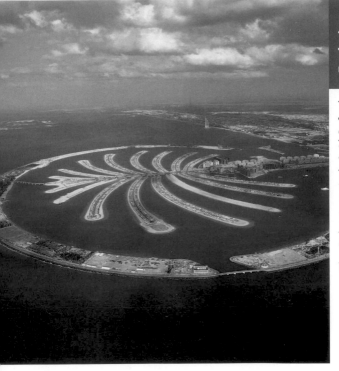

The Palm Jumeirah & Al Sufouh

If you only do one thing in...

Palm Jumeirah & Al Sufouh

Take in the (recreated) old Arabia by wandering around Souk Madinat Jumeirah's alleyways before heading to the beach for a view of the Burj Al Arab.

Best for...

Eating & Drinking: Sip with a view at Après while watching people hurtle down Ski Dubai's slopes.

Families: Head to Atlantis' water attractions to kick back on the lazy river, watch the dolphins or stretch out on the hotel's private beach.

Relaxation: Pamper in the incredible luxury of Talise Spa at Al Qasr Hotel, Madinat Jumeirah.

Shopping: Mall of the Emirates is a major 'New Dubai' dining and entertainment hub – and it also has some of the region's best shopping.

Sightseeing: Take a ride on the Palm's monorail, which provides great views of the coastline, plus the chance to nosey at some of the island's villas.

Clockwise from top: Al Mahara, Souk Madinat Jumeirah, Dubai's icons

Umm Hurair: Creekside

Once known as the leisure capital of the city, people now flock to this area for luxury shopping, lazy afternoons and family fun.

Together, Oud Metha, Umm Hurair and Zabeel form a park-filled corner of Dubai that lines the bottom half of the creek. Wafi and Lamcy Plaza are popular shopping spots both for bargains and international fashion labels, while the pyramid-shaped Raffles Dubai hotel has several top-notch dining options.

Children's City

04 334 0808
childrencity.ae

Gate 1, Creek Park, Umm Hurair 2

Children's City offers kids hands-on educational amusement facilities. There's a planetarium, a nature centre, and the Discovery Space, revealing the miracles of the human body. It is aimed at five to 12 year olds, although toddlers and teenagers – or even adults – may also find it entertaining.
Map 4 C5 **Metro** Healthcare City

Creek Park

04 336 7633
dm.gov.ae

Riyadh St, Umm Hurair 2

Creek Park is blessed with acres of gardens, fishing piers, barbecue sites, children's play areas and kiosks. Running along the park's 2.5km stretch of creek frontage is a cable car

Umm Hurair and Dubai Creek

system, allowing visitors an unrestricted view from 30m in the air. Entrance costs Dhs.5.

Map 4 C6 **Metro** Oud Metha

Zabeel Park

04 398 6888

Shk Rashid Rd, Al Kifaf

dm.gov.ae

Providing an oasis of greenery in dusty Dubai, Zabeel Park has several recreational areas, a jogging track, a mini cricket pitch, a football field, a boating lake and an amphitheatre, plus a number of kiosks serving snacks. Entry costs Dhs.5.

Map 4 A3 **Metro** Al Jafiliya

MAKE UP FOR EVER

If you only do one thing in...
Umm Hurair

Sample the joys of shopping, spas and oversized cocktails all under one roof at Wafi.

Best for...

Eating & Drinking: There are plenty of top restaurants at Wafi, but the modern Indian cuisine of Asha's truly captures the imagination.

Families: Let the kids loose at Children's City – great fun for adults too.

Relaxation: Take a picnic to Creek Park and watch the park and creek action unfold.

Shopping: Find unforgettable gifts at the underground souk of Khan Murjan.

Sightseeing: Squeeze into a cable car in Creek Park for great views over the water.

Clockwise from top: Raffles, Wafi, Creek Park

Off The Beaten Track

Some of Dubai's funkier cultural hotspots are found in some of the most unlikely places.

Outside of the areas already covered in this chapter, some sightseeing highlights are dotted around other parts of town. The area of Karama is famous for its markets and restaurants, serving cheap south-Asian dinners; Satwa is home to some of the best people-watching in the city, and the dusty industrial park, Al Qouz, hosts several of the most cutting-edge art galleries in the region.

Gallery Isabelle Van Den Eynde

04 323 5052

Alserkal Ave, 8th St, Al Qouz Industrial 1   ivde.net

This progressive art gallery represents Middle Eastern artists and is partnered with galleries in Europe. The result is a hub where collectors can source artwork and get advice on everything from finance to framing. Even if you're not in the market to buy, there are exhibitions by a steadily growing roster of talent. Open 10am to 7pm Saturday to Thursday. **Map** 1 E3 **Metro** Noor Bank

Global Village

04 362 4114

Shk Mohd Bin Zayed Rd, Wadi Al Safa 4   globalvillage.ae

Between October and March a huge plot of paved desert outside of Dubai blossoms into a celebration of multiculturalism and fairground fun. There are plenty of big

rides and action-orientated shows to entertain the family, but the main attraction is the shopping. Vendors come from over 45 countries in Africa, Asia and the Middle East to showcase their cultural wares. Much of the clothing, furniture and decorations on sale are less-than-attractive, but each area has shops full of knick-knacks you can't find anywhere else.
Map 1 E6

Iranian Mosque
04 344 2886
Al Wasl St, Jumeira 1
3rdimam.com
Non-Muslims can't enter the Iranian Mosque, but it's still worth admiring (and photographing) from the outside. The blue mosaic tiling, pillars, arches and elaborate minarets are typical of Persian architecture, making this one of the most photogenic sights in Dubai. The mosque also serves as a stunning counterpoint to some of the modern places of worship you'll see elsewhere in the city.
Map 1 H2 **Metro** World Trade Centre

The jamjar
04 341 7303
Nr Dubai Garden Centre,
17A St, Al Qouz Industrial 3
thejamjardubai.com
The jamjar is injecting a little culture to Sheikh Zayed Road. This small, bright gallery offers wannabe Picassos the chance to let their creative juices flow. Everything from paints to brushes and canvases is provided and prices start from Dhs.195. Open 10am to 8pm Monday to Thursday and Saturday, 2pm to 8pm on Friday and closed Sunday.
Map 1 E3 **Metro** First Gulf Bank

Karama

Primarily a residential area consisting of relatively low-cost flats in low-rise apartment blocks, Karama is well known for having something for everyone. It has a great shopping area, which is particularly notorious for its imitation goods, and the popular Karama Complex. Karama's merchants are a far cry from their mall counterparts and offer a challenge if you like practising your haggling skills. There's a great range of inexpensive restaurants serving tasty Indian and Pakistani cuisine, including Saravana Bhavan and Karachi Darbar (04 334 7272).
Map 5 A4 **Metro** ADCB

Opera Gallery

04 323 0909

Gate Village Bldg 3
 DIFC, Zaa'beel 2

operagallery.com

Part of an international chain, Opera Gallery opened in 2008 in Dubai International Financial Centre. It has a permanent collection of art on display and for sale, mainly European and Chinese, with visiting exhibitions changing throughout the year. The permanent collection also includes several masterpieces, so look out for the odd Dali or Picasso.
Map 2 D2 **Metro** Financial Centre

Plant Street

Al Hudaiba St, Al Satwa

Famous for pots and plants, pet shops, fabric shops and hardware outlets, Plant Street is another spot that hasn't changed much since the beginning of Dubai's boom. Head here on a Saturday evening to soak up the atmosphere, but

Global Village

women are advised to cover up (no miniskirts, shorts or strappy t-shirts) to avoid being stared at.
Map 1 H2 **Metro** Trade Centre

The Third Line

04 341 1367

Nr Times Square, Al Qouz Industrial 1   thethirdline.com

One of the leading lights of the Dubai art scene, The Third Line gallery in Al Qouz hosts exhibitions by artists originating from or working in the Middle East. There are indoor and outdoor spaces for shows, many of which have caught the eye of both local and international collectors. The gallery is open Saturday to Thursday 10am to 7pm; it is closed on Fridays. **Map** 1 F3 **Metro** Noor Bank

Further Out

The United Arab Emirates offers visitors some spectacular sights, from modern cities to ancient forts, and mountain pools to seemingly infinite deserts.

If you've time, hire a car or book a tour and hit the road: there's a lot to see, and many sights are just a short drive away. Close to Dubai, nature lovers should check out Ras Al Khor Wildlife Sanctuary (Ras Al Khor Road, 04 606 6822), the only nature reserve within the city and a great place for bird watchers, with 1,500 flamingos. You'll quickly be surrounded by rolling sand dunes, wandering camels and imposing mountains. Heading out of Dubai to the other cities and emirates can be hugely rewarding and will add a worthy cultural perspective to your time in the UAE.

Abu Dhabi

Dubai is sometimes mistaken as the capital of the UAE, but that honour actually belongs to Abu Dhabi. Oil was discovered there before Dubai (1958 compared with 1966) and today it accounts for 10% of the world's known crude oil reserves, making it one of the richest cities on earth. It is home to a growing number of renowned hotels, a selection of shiny shopping malls and a sprinkling of culture in the form of heritage sites, souks and the upcoming Abu Dhabi Guggenheim and Louvre galleries. Don't miss the 22,000sq m Sheikh Zayed Grand Mosque (szgmc.ae).

EXPERIENCE THE WORLD'S FIRST FERRARI-BRANDED THEME PARK

Welcome to Ferrari World Abu Dhabi, the largest indoor theme park in the world where the passion and innovation of Ferrari fuel rides and attractions for the entire family. Immerse yourself in unforgettable experiences as you brave the world's fastest rollercoaster, soar virtually over Italy, enjoy a 4D adventure, admire the largest collection of Ferraris outside Maranello, indulge in Italian and international dining choices, and find a souvenir at the world's largest Ferrari Store.

Don't stand in line, book online.

STAY CONNECTED WITH US

FERRARIWORLDABUDHABI.COM

FIND YOUR DRIVE

Emirates Palace (kempinski.com) is another must-do: the stunning hotel houses several excellent restaurants and is well worth the visit for the architecture alone. Off the coast, Yas Island is a thrill-seeker's delight: in addition to the annual Formula 1 race, other events and driving experiences take place year-round at Yas Marina Circuit, while Ferrari World Abu Dhabi theme park (ferrariworldabudhabi.com), features petrol-fumed attractions of every kind and Yas Waterworld (yaswaterworld.com), a huge water park, offers aquatic thrills. The stunning Yas Marina is worth a visit, while the nearby du Arena and du Forum play host regularly to concerts and events. You can stay at the luxurious Yas Viceroy, play golf at Yas Links Golf Club, dine at the restaurants in the Yas Plaza group of hotels and chill on Yas Beach. Yas Mall opened in late 2014 at an impressive 2.5 million square foot, making it the second largest mall in the UAE.

Nearby Saadiyat Island is a holiday paradise with a handful of classy hotels and resorts that include the luxurious Saadiyat Beach Club (saadiyatbeachclub.ae).

South-west of Abu Dhabi is the Liwa Oasis, where the spectacular dunes are a photographer's dream. Liwa lies at the edge of the Rub Al Khali (Empty Quarter), one of the largest sand deserts in the world.

Al Ain

Al Ain is a fertile oasis that sits on ancient trading routes between Oman and the Gulf. The birthplace of the late, revered Sheikh Zayed, Al Ain is known as the Garden City, full of date plantations and pockets of greenery. These oases are lovely places to explore; drive around the networks of walled, cobbled roads, park up, and wander through the lush green plantations. You might even get to taste some fresh fruit if you stumble across some harvested bounty (be sure to ask permission from the picker before you pop one in your mouth). Next to the main Al Ain Oasis is the interesting Al Ain Palace Museum (03 751 7755, abudhabi.ae), which illustrates aspects of life in the UAE. Al Ain Zoo (03 799 2000, alainzoo. ae) is a nature-lover's dream and easily one of the city's best attractions. Conservation is the keyword here, with natural habitats recreated to be as near to the real thing as possible, and you can get the whole family up close to animals including giraffes, zebras and rhinos. For a great view over the city and desert landscape, take a scenic drive up Jebel Hafeet. The winding road rises to the summit, where you'll find the Mercure Grand Jebel Hafeet Hotel – a great place for a refreshing drink with a terrific view (03 783 8888, mercure. com). At the foothill of the mountain is Wadi Adventure (wadiadventure.ae), which offers a range of adrenaline-pumping activities such as whitewater rafting and kayaking.

East Coast

Even if you're only in the UAE for a short time, a trip to the east coast is a must. You can get there in less than two hours.

The diving is considered better than that off Dubai's coast, mainly because of increased visibility. Snoopy Island off Dibba's coast is a favourite spot for snorkelling. The east coast is home to a few interesting areas, many of which are free to explore. The site of the oldest mosque in the UAE, Bidiyah, is roughly half way down the coast, north of Khor Fakkan. The building is believed to date back to the middle of the 15th century and was restored in 2003. The village is considered one of the oldest settlements on the east coast, which is thought to have been inhabited since 3,000BC. Located at the northernmost point of the coast, Dibba is made up of three fishing villages, each coming under a different jurisdiction: Sharjah, Fujairah, and Oman. The villages share an attractive bay and excellent diving locations. The Hajar Mountains provide a wonderful backdrop to the public beaches. Further north across the border into Oman is Khasab, a great base for exploring the inlets and unspoilt waters of Musandam. You can stay at the Atana Khasab (+968 2 673 0777, atanahotels. com), which can organise dhow cruises and dolphin watching, or at the luxurious Six Senses Zighy Bay (+968 2 673 5555, sixsenses.com).

Further south on the coast lies Fujairah, the youngest of the seven emirates. Overlooking the atmospheric old town is a 300-year old fort. The surrounding hillsides are dotted with more such ancient forts and watchtowers, which add an air of mystery and charm. Dubai residents often use Fujairah as a base for exploring the rest of the coast. Hotels include Le Meridien Al Aqah Beach Resort (09 244 9000, lemeridien-alaqah.com), and Radisson Blu Resort, Fujairah (09 244 9700, radissonblu.com). Khor Kalba sits just south of Fujairah. It's the most northerly mangrove forest in the world, and home to a variety of plant, marine and birdlife not found anywhere else in the UAE. A canoe tour by Desert Rangers is the best way to reach the heart of the reserve.

Hatta

The road leading to Hatta from Dubai (E44) is a trip in itself. Watch as the sand gradually changes from beige to dark orange and then disappears, only to be replaced by jagged mountains. The famous Big Red sand dune lies on this road, and is a popular spot for dune driving in 4WDs or quad bikes.

Hatta is a small town, nestled at the foot of the Hajar Mountains, about 100km from Dubai city and 10km from the Dubai-Oman border. It is home to the oldest fort in Dubai emirate, which was built in 1790. You'll also see several watchtowers on the surrounding hills. On the drive you'll pass a row of carpet shops, ideal for putting your bargaining skills into practice. The town itself has a sleepy, relaxed feel, and includes the Heritage Village (04 852 1374), which charts the area's 3,000 year history and includes a 200 year-old mosque and the fortress built by Sheikh Maktoum bin Hasher Al Maktoum in 1896, which is now used as a weaponry museum.

The Hatta Fort Hotel's (04 809 9333, jaresortshotels.com) bungalow-style rooms feature stunning Arabic decor and the resort has plenty of sports and leisure facilities, including shooting and mini-golf.

Beyond the village and into the mountains are the Hatta Pools, where you can see deep, strangely shaped canyons carved out by rushing floodwater.

The trail towards the pools is graded, so a two-wheel drive car and some skilled driving should be enough to get you there. To get to the pools from the Dubai-Hatta road, take a right at the fort roundabout, then left towards the Heritage Village, another left at the roundabout, and then the first main right. After driving through a second village, the tarmac will end and you will see a gravel track on your right.

Northern Emirates

North of Dubai and Sharjah are Ajman, Umm Al Quwain and Ras Al Khaimah. These three emirates are much smaller in size than Dubai and Abu Dhabi and are also less developed.

Ajman is the smallest of the emirates, but its proximity to Dubai and Sharjah has enabled it to grow considerably. It was once known as one of the largest dhow building centres in the region, and while it is mainly modern boats that emerge from the yards these days, you can still catch a glimpse of a traditionally built dhow sailing out to sea. Ajman also has some great beaches and a pleasant corniche. Much of the nightlife revolves around the Ajman Kempinski Hotel & Resort (06 714 5555, kempinski.com).

Umm Al Quwain has the smallest population and little has changed over the years, though it is home to the expansive Dreamland Aqua Park (dreamlanduae.com). Two of the most interesting activities Umm Al Quwain has to offer are crab hunting and mangrove tours. The Flamingo Beach Resort (06 765 0000, flamingoresort.ae) offers both.

Ras Al Khaimah is north of Dubai and you can make the trip in around an hour on the Emirates Road. With the jagged Hajar Mountains rising behind the city, and the Arabian Gulf stretching out from the shore, RAK has some of the best scenery in the UAE. A creek divides the city into the old town and the newer Al Nakheel district. For a day trip, you should go to the souk in the old town and the National Museum of Ras

Al Khaimah (07 233 3411, rakheritage.rak.ae). This is a good starting point for exploring the surrounding countryside and visiting the ancient sites of Ghalilah and Shimal. RAK also has plenty of watersports – check out RAK Sailing Academy.

Sharjah

Before Dubai's rise to prominence as a trading and tourism hotspot, neighbouring Sharjah was one of the wealthiest towns in the region, with settlers earning their livelihood from fishing, pearling and trade. Sharjah's commitment to art, culture and preserving its traditional heritage is well known throughout the Arab world and the city is home to several museums that are well worth a visit; see sharjahmuseums.ae for full details of these.

Sharjah is built around Khalid Lagoon (popularly known as the creek), and the surrounding Buhairah Corniche is a popular spot for an evening stroll. From various points on the lagoon, small dhows can be hired to see the lights of the city from the water. The Heritage Area is a fascinating old walled city, home to numerous museums and the traditional Souk Al Arsah. The nearby Arts Area is a treat for art lovers with galleries and more museums. A must is Al Qasba (06 556 0777, alqasba.ae), which has performance spaces and waterside restaurants. Another worthy stop-off is the Sharjah Natural History & Botanical Museum (06 531 1999, epaashj. com). Shoppers shouldn't miss the beautiful Central Souk, also known as the Blue Souk. The two buildings contain more than 600 shops selling gold and knick-knacks. This is one of the best places in the UAE to buy carpets.

Oman

Just a few hours from Dubai, you'll find the countless attractions of Oman. It's a peaceful and breathtaking country, with history, culture and spectacular scenery. The capital, Muscat, has enough attractions to keep you busy for a short break, including beautiful beaches, some great restaurants and cafes, and the mesmerising old souk at Mutrah. Out of the capital, you will find many historic old towns and forts, and some of the most stunning mountain and wadi scenery in the region. Salalah in the south has the added bonus of being cool and wet in the summer. Isolated from the rest of the country, on the tip of the Arabian Peninsula, is the Omani enclave of Musandam. With its jagged mountains and fjord-like inlets, it has the moniker 'the Norway of the Middle East' and is a must-visit if you are in Dubai for any serious length of time.

Ras Al Jinz is a small fishing village on the Ras Al Hadd Turtle Reserve. The protected beach is where endangered green turtles come to nest and visitors can see the huge turtles by booking a guided tour with Ras Al Jinz Scientific & Visitor Center (+968 9 655 0606/0707, rasaljinz-turtlereserve. com) which has a small guesthouse, restaurant and gift shop.

A flight from Dubai to Muscat takes 45 minutes, but when you factor in check-in times and customs it's not much quicker than driving. There are daily flights from Dubai with Emirates and Oman Air, while Air Arabia flies from Sharjah. Regular flights to Salalah from Dubai are also available. It is possible to drive to Musandam from Dubai in around three hours, but make sure your hire car insurance covers Oman. For further information see the *Oman Residents' & Visitors' Guide*.

Whitewashed buildings of Muscat

Tours & Sightseeing

Whether it be by plane, boat or 4WD, taking a tour is a fun and efficient way to see a different side of the UAE.

Navigating the city by taxi or metro can be pretty easy, but exploring the surrounding areas often proves a bit more difficult without the help of a guide. Boat tours are a great way to see the city from afar while enjoying the clear Gulf waters; helicopter and plane tours give the most extensive look at the growing city; and bus tours offer plenty of information and more user-friendly schedules.

No visitor should leave without experiencing a desert safari of some sort. Expert drivers blast 4WDs up, down and around massive dunes while passing old Bedouin villages and pointing out incredible natural attractions. Mountain safaris lead passengers through the narrow wadis of the Hajar Mountains. Most driving safaris include pickup from your hotel and lunch. Some end the day of driving at a replica Bedouin camp, where passengers can watch a belly dancer, eat Arabic delicacies and smoke shisha. Some operators run overnight safaris that combine half-day treks with a driving adventure.

While most of the companies listed on page 144 offer a wide range of experiences, some are more specialised. Both Aerogulf Services and Seawings concentrate on plane tours, Balloon Adventures is the city's main balloon ride operator, Big Bus Tours is the premier bus tour provider, and Bristol Middle East concentrates on boat and yacht tours.

Life is **a safari,**
let's conquer it **together**

netours
Leading the way...

Tour Operators

Absolute Adventure	04 392 6463	adventure.ae
Aerogulf Services Company	04 877 6120	aerogulfservices.com
Alpha Tours	04 294 9888	alphatoursdubai.com
Arabian Adventures	04 343 9966	arabian-adventures.com
Balloon Adventures Emirates	04 285 4949	ballooning.ae
Big Bus Tours	04 340 7709	bigbustours.com
Bristol Middle East Yacht Solution	04 366 3538	bristol-middleeast.com
Desert Adventures	04 450 4450	desertadventures.com
Desert Rangers	04 456 9944	desertrangers.com
Dubai Tourism & Travel Services	04 336 7727	dubai-travel.ae
Gulf Ventures > *p.143*	04 404 5880	gulfventures.com
Knight Tours	04 343 7725	knighttours.ae
Net Tours > *p.141*	04 376 2333	nettoursuae.com
Oasis Palm Tourism	04 262 8889	opdubai.com
Omeir Travel Agency	04 337 7727	omeir.com
Orient Tours	04 282 8238	orient-tours-uae.com
Seawings	04 807 0708	seawings.ae
Sunflower Tours	04 334 5554	sunflowerdubai.com
Tour Dubai	04 336 8407	tour-dubai.com
Travco	04 336 6643	travcotravel.ae
Wonder Bus Tours	04 359 5656	wonderbustours.net

Think you know Dubai?
Wait till you experience it with us.

We've been thrilling visitors to the United Emirates and Oman for over two decades. Off-road desert action; polo and golf to camel-trekking and sandboarding; incredible rides by balloon and sea-plane; wedding celebrations and days that end in the romance of our Bedouin desert camp. All of this tailored to groups, families, couples or solo travellers-and wrapped in luxurious hospitality.

Call us today and discover why Gulf Ventures is your natural partner.

Use the booking code **EG2015** to get an exclusive **10% discount** on any desert experience

T: +971 4 404 5880
E: tours@gulfventures.com

gulfventures.com
Leisure Services / Event Services / Tours & Excursions

GULF VENTURES
Destination Management Specialists

Sports & Spas

Active Dubai	146
Sports & Activities	148
Spectator Sports	160
Out of Dubai	164
Spas	166

Active Dubai

Dubai has a wealth of spas, sports and resorts dedicated to the art of relaxation.

It is not just shops and beaches that attract visitors to Dubai. Numerous world-class sporting events take place in the city throughout the year, drawing crowds of residents and tourists alike. The Dubai World Cup is the richest horse race in the world, the Dubai Rugby Sevens regularly pulls in crowds in excess of 70,000 and the Dubai Duty Free Tennis Championships see the world's leading players compete in an intimate setting.

Dubai is also home to several excellent golf courses, many designed by leading figures such as Robert Trent Jones II, Colin Montgomerie and Nick Faldo.

Traditional Arabian sports, such as camel racing and falconry, offer an interesting perspective on local heritage, and should not be missed.

A combination of Arabian Gulf shoreline and the vast expanses of desert just outside the city make Dubai a great adventure sports destination: from kitesurfing and diving to dune driving and sand skiing, there are many opportunities for unique and exciting sports activities.

All this activity aside, those who are seeking blissful holidays spent relaxing and rejuvenating will find a collection of world-class spas offering a range of unique treatments in luxurious surroundings, usually at surprisingly reasonable prices.

Clockwise from top left: climbing Fossil Rock, underwater life, Dubai Tennis Championships

Miles of sand dunes, clear seas, classic Arabian heritage and superb sports facilities: holidays in Dubai are packed with unique sporting opportunities.

Dhow Charters

Al Boom Tourist Village

04 324 3000

Shk Rashid Rd, Umm Hurair 2 · · · · · · · · · · · · · · · alboom.ae

Al Boom Tourist Village operates nine dhow boats on the creek, ranging from single-deckers with room for 20 people, right up to the huge triple-decker Mumtaz, which can take 300 passengers. It offers a variety of packages, with prices varying accordingly. As well as the usual dinner cruises, late-night trips can also be arranged.

Map 4 C6 **Metro** Healthcare City

Khasab Travel & Tours

04 266 9950

Warba Centre, Al Muraqqabat · · · · · · · · · · khasabtours.com

This operator organises day cruises in Khasab, Oman (including car transfers from Dubai). The route follows the rugged Musandam coastline, which has been dubbed the 'Norway of Arabia,' offering fantastic photo opportunities: you'll pass small fishing villages in incredibly remote locations and will (hopefully) also see dolphins and turtles. Prices start at Dhs.200 per adult for a full day, including lunch and refreshments. **Map** 4 E4 **Metro** Abu Baker Al Siddique

Golf

With an ideal climate for most of the year, golf is a popular sport in Dubai and the number of international-standard courses has increased rapidly. Although plans for a Tiger Woods designed course were cancelled, recent additions to Dubai's golf scene include courses designed by such names as South Africa's 'Big Easy' Ernie Els. Dubai Golf operates a central reservation system at dubaigolf.com.

Al Badia Golf Club By InterContinental Dubai Festival City

04 601 0101

Dubai Festival City, Al Kheeran   albadiagolfclub.ae

World-renowned golf course designer Robert Trent Jones II is behind the InterContinental's offering. Lying at the heart of Dubai Festival City, beside the creek, the resort enjoys great views across the city. The 7,303 yard par 72 Championship Course has a plush clubhouse and extensive water features.

Map 1 J4 **Metro** Emirates

Arabian Ranches Golf Club

04 366 3000

Shk Mhd Bin Zayed Rd, Arabian Ranches,
  Wadi Al Safa 6   arabianranchesgolfdubai.com

Designed by Ian Baker-Finch in association with Nicklaus Design, this par 72 grass course uses the natural desert terrain and features indigenous shrubs and bushes. You must have an official handicap to play, but can reserve a tee-off time six days in advance. Facilities include a golf academy with floodlit driving range, an extensive short game practice area, and GPS on all golf carts. **Map** 1 D5

Dubai Creek Golf & Yacht Club   04 295 6000

Nr Deira City Centre, Baniyas St,
  Port Saeed   dubaigolf.com

The par 71 course was designed by Thomas Björn and is open
to all players with a valid handicap certificate. Those who are
new to the game are encouraged to train with PGA qualified
instructors at the academy. There is also a nine-hole par three
course, a floodlit range and extensive short game practice
areas. The iconic clubhouse features several dining favourites
and two pro shops. **Map** 4 C6 **Metro** Deira City Centre

The Els Club Dubai   04 425 1010

Dubai Sports City, Al Hebiah 4   elsclubdubai.com

Designed by Ernie Els, this 18-hole course that stretches
7,538 yards is very popular among Dubai's golfers. A massive
Mediterranean clubhouse is still under construction, but a
temporary clubhouse serves members and visitors in the
meantime. **Map** 1 C4 **Metro** Dubai Internet City

Emirates Golf Club   04 417 9999

Off Sheikh Zayed Rd, Emirates Living,
  Al Thanyah 3   dubaigolf.com

At Emirates Golf Club you can choose from two 18 hole
courses: the 7,301 yard, par 72 Majlis Course – the first grass
course in the Middle East and venue for the Dubai Desert
Classic – or the Faldo Course designed by Nick Faldo and IMG
Design. The club has a Peter Cowen Golf Academy, along with
two driving ranges, practice areas and clubhouse.
Map 3 B2 **Metro** Nakheel

JA Jebel Ali Golf Resort

04 814 5555

Nr Palm Jebel Ali, Jabal Ali jaresortshotels.com

Situated in the landscaped gardens of the JA Jebel Ali Golf Resort & Spa, this nine-hole, par 36 course offers views of the Arabian Gulf. Renowned for its good condition all year, the course is also home to the Jebel Ali Golf Resort & Spa Challenge, the opener for the Omega Dubai Desert Classic.

Montgomerie Golf Club

04 390 5600

The Address Montgomerie Dubai,
Emirates Living, Al Thanyah 4 themontgomerie.com

Designed by Colin Montgomerie and Desmond Muirhead, the 18 hole, par 72 course has some unique characteristics, including the 656 yard 18th hole. The facilities include a driving range and a swing analysis studio.

Map 3 B3 **Metro** Nakheel

Hot Air Ballooning & Parasailing

Balloon Adventures Emirates (04 285 4949), Amigos Balloons (04 289 9295, amigos-balloons.com) and Desert Rangers (04 456 9944) offer trips across the desert in a hot air balloon. Journeys with Amigos Balloons cost Dhs.950 per person and set off from a variety of locations – you can also go for a private flight for two for Dhs.5,500. If you'd like an aerial view of the Palm Jumeirah but can't afford a balloon, then try parasailing. The Sheraton Jumeirah Beach Resort (04 399 5533) has a watersports and an activity centre, and Nautica 1992 (050 426 2415) operates from the Habtoor Grand. Summertime Marine Sports (04 257 3084) also offers flights from the open beach near Le Meridien Mina Seyahi hotel (04 399 3333). All use specially designed boats with winches and a launch pad on the back, so you don't have to sprint down the beach to get airborne. You can expect to pay around Dhs.250 for a 15 to 20 minute ride or Dhs.350 for the tandem option – however, prices vary depending on the length and option of the ride.

Motorsports

The UAE deserts provide ideal locations for rallying, and many events are organised throughout the year by the Emirates Motor Sports Federation (emsf.ae). The high-profile Abu Dhabi Desert Challenge (abudhabidesertchallenge.com) is one of the top events in World Cup Cross Country Rallying. Other events throughout the year include the Spring Desert Rally (4WD), Peace Rally (saloons), Jeep Jamboree (safari), Drakkar Noir 1000 Dunes Rally (4WD), Shell Festival Parade, Audi Driving Skills (driving challenge) and Federation Rally (4WD). Yas Island (yasisland.ae), located a short drive away in Abu Dhabi, is home to various attractions and amenities to delight any petrolhead. In addition to the annual Formula 1 Etihad Airways Grand Prix, the Yas Marina Circuit (yasmarinacircuit.com) hosts several other motorsports events throughout the year. Also on Yas Island, theme park Ferrari World Abu Dhabi (ferrariworldabudhabi.com) features all manner of high-octane attractions.

Dubai Autodrome
Dubai Motor City, Al Hebiah 1

04 367 8700
dubaiautodrome.com

The Dubai Autodrome (part of Dubailand) is the home of motorsport in Dubai. It has six different track configurations,

What would you like to be today?
Over 80 professions to choose from!

Get Ready for a Better World!

In KidZania, children can understand the world of grown-ups better through activities based on role-playing. A child can become a chef, surgeon, radio host, firefighter and a whole lot more, all in the course of a day.

Bring your children to KidZania. Let them be adults for a day!

KidZania
Dubai

LEVEL 2 | THE DUBAI MALL

including a 5.39km FIA-sanctioned GP circuit, premium pit facilities and a 7,000 seat grandstand. The venue hosts events throughout the year, including rounds of the FIA GT Championships. You can experience the thrill of driving on a racetrack with the guidance of qualified instructors. A range of packages and experiences are offered, including a track taster session in Audi TTs with prices starting from Dhs.825. Wannabe Vettels of any age can burn rubber at the kartdrome. After a safety briefing, you'll take to your powerful 390cc kart (there are smaller 120cc karts for the kids) and hit the tarmac on the exciting 1.2km circuit. **Map** 1 D5

Skiing & Snowboarding

Escape the heat and glide over Dubai's Olympic-sized ice rink in The Dubai Mall (dubaiicerink.com). Public sessions last two hours and start at Dhs.55 with skate hire. Or visit Ski Dubai (04 409 4090) – the first indoor ski resort in the Middle East, housed in the Mall of the Emirates. It's home to five slopes from beginner slopes to the world's first indoor 'black' run. If you don't ski, you can roll down the slope inside a giant inflatable ball or zipline on the new Snow Bullet. The attractions also include the opportunity to meet the cute resident penguins. The slope has chair lifts and tow lifts, and there's a shop selling boards, and clothing. Strict rules ensure only skilled skiers and boarders can hit the slopes, but beginners can book a lesson. Entrance to the Snow Park is Dhs.140 for adults and Dhs.130 for children. Prices for a two-hour Ski Slope Pass start at Dhs.200 for adults and Dhs.170 for kids; the prices include equipment and clothing (except gloves).

Wadi & Dune Bashing

Most car rental agencies offer visitors 4WDs capable of desert driving. If renting a 4WD, make sure you get the details of the insurance plan, as many rental insurers won't cover damage caused by off-roading. Dune bashing, or desert driving, is one of the toughest challenges for both car and driver, but once you have mastered it, it's a lot of fun.

If you do venture out into the desert, it is a good idea to have at least one experienced driver and one other car to help tow you out if you get stuck. Most major tour companies offer a range of desert and mountain safaris if you'd rather leave the driving to the professionals.

Driving in wadis is usually a bit more straightforward. Wadis are (usually) dry gullies, carved through the rock by rushing floodwaters, following the course of seasonal rivers. The main safety precaution to take when wadi bashing is to keep your eyes open for rare, but not impossible, thunder storms developing. The wadis can fill up quickly and you will need to make your way to higher ground pretty fast to avoid flash floods. For further information and tips on off-road driving in the UAE, check out the *UAE Off-Road Explorer*.

Watersports & Diving

Most beachside hotels offer watersports to guests and visitors, including sea kayaking, sailing and windsurfing. Non-guests may have to pay beach fees to access the facilities, though sometimes you can enter the beach area for free if you make a prior reservation. Contact the Habtoor Grand Resort (04 399 5000) and Le Meridien Mina Seyahi (04 399 3333) for pricing

The Dubai sports scene is amazingly varied

and availability of various watersports – both are located along the 1.7km beach in JBR. You'll find parasailing, kayaking, windsurfing, dinghies and banana boats.

Sea Riders (055 510 3739, searidersuae.com) also offers watersports including wake-boarding, yacht charter, fishing and tailor-made daytrips.

Simulated Fun

Dubai's malls have fantastic entertainment; try sky diving at Playnation, Mirdif City Centre or for the biggest selection, head to SEGA Republic at The Dubai Mall, which has motor racing, a jungle safari and a bobsleigh simulator for big (and little) kids to try.

Diving is popular and the clear waters off the coast are home to a variety of marine species, coral life and even shipwrecks. You'll see some exotic fish and possibly moray eels, small sharks, barracudas, sea snakes and stingrays.

Most of the wrecks are located on the west coast of the UAE, while the flora and fauna can be seen on the east side, in Fujairah. Another option for diving enthusiasts is a trip to Musandam. Part of the Sultanate of Oman, it is often described as the 'Norway of the Middle East' due to its many inlets and cliffs that plunge directly into the sea. Sheer wall dives with strong currents and clear waters are more suitable for advanced divers, while the huge bays with their calm waters and bountiful shallow reefs are ideal for the less experienced. Courses are offered under the usual international training organisations. More details on specific dives and sites can be found in the *UAE Diving* book.

Al Boom Diving

Al Wasl St, Jumeira 1

04 342 2993
alboomdiving.com

Al Boom Diving is a purpose-built school with a fully outfitted diving shop. A variety of courses are held both here and at the company's PADI Gold Palm Resort at Le Meridien Al Aqah Beach Resort (09 244 9000) near Fujairah on the East Coast. For aquatic thrills right in the heart of the city, Al Boom Diving also offers the chance to dive with the sharks in The Dubai Mall's gigantic aquarium.

Map 1 H2 **Metro** Emirates Towers

Pavilion Dive Centre

Jumeirah Beach Hotel, Umm Suqeim 3

04 406 8828
jumeirah.com

This centre is run by PADI course directors, who offer courses for beginners through to instructors. Daily dive charters for certified divers are available in Dubai, and trips to the Musandam peninsula in Oman can be organised on request. Two dives with full equipment are priced at Dhs.450 in Dubai or Dhs.700 in Musandam (including transport and lunch).

Map 3 E1 **Metro** Mall of the Emirates

Wadi Adventure

Jebel Hafeet, Al Ain

03 781 8422
wadiadventure.ae

Located on the foothills of Al Ain's Jebel Hafeet mountain, this new resort is worth the 90 minute car ride from Dubai if you're a fan of adrenaline-pumping watersports. In addition to three world-class white water rafting and kayaking runs, there's also a huge surf pool. Entry costs Dhs.50, activities are charged separately.

Spectator Sports

Dubai has the best line-up of international sport in the region, with world-class tennis, golf and horse racing among the highlights.

A good range of sporting events is organised in Dubai and the emirate is steadily backing more big international events that not only capture the local imagination, but also draw sporting enthusiasts from around the world. A big advantage is that crowds are smaller and tickets for larger events are more freely available than they would be in other countries, though you'll have to be quick. Horse racing, desert rallies and motorsports are very popular as are local sports like camel racing.

Camel Racing

This is a chance to see a truly traditional local sport. Races take place in the winter months and additional games are often held on public holidays. Races were previously held at the track at

Camel Rides

Take a short camel ride along the beach near the Hilton Dubai Jumeirah or as part of a desert safari – it's a great way to experience this traditional mode of transport. The lumbering clumsiness of the camel standing up when you first hop on forms a marked contrast to the surprising smoothness of the ride itself.

Nadd Al Shiba, but this has closed to make way for Meydan City. To find the new location, head up the Al Ain Road, past the Dubai Outlet Mall, until you reach the Al Lisali exit. Turn right off this exit and you will see the track on your right. Races are usually held early on a Friday morning, but you should see camels being exercised during the day in the cooler months.

Golf

DP World Tour Championship

Jumeirah Golf Estates   europeantour.com

The Dubai World Championship is the grand finale of The Race to Dubai, the European Tour's season-long competition which features 50 tournaments in 27 destinations. This annual tournament runs for four days and is open to the leading 60 players in The Race to Dubai rankings after the 49th event, ensuring that the cream of the golf world qualifies for the chance to compete for a prize fund of $8 million. **Map** 1 B4

Omega Dubai Desert Classic   04 380 2112

Emirates Golf Club   dubaidesertclassic.com

One of the highlights of the Dubai sporting calendar, this European PGA Tour competition is a popular winter event among both players and spectators. The tournament takes place at the end of January and start of February; see the website for more details. Top golfers who have previously competed in the event include Tiger Woods, Ernie Els and Henrik Stenson. **Map** 3 B2 **Metro** Nakheel

Horse Racing

Dubai Racing Club
04 327 0077

Meydan Racecourse,
Nadd Al Shiba 1
dubairacingclub.com

A visit to Dubai during the winter months is not complete without experiencing race night. For the past few years, the races have taken place at the impressively large, state-of-the-art racecourse in Meydan City. Featuring a 60,000 seat grandstand, a five-star hotel and several restaurants, it's as much a racecourse as an entertainment destination in its own right. Every March, the world's richest horse race, the Dubai World Cup, takes place here. You can see a slightly more raw form of horse racing at Jebel Ali racecourse (04 347 4914), near The Greens. **Map** 1 G4

Motorsports

Since 2009, Abu Dhabi has been hosting an annual Formula 1 World Championship, held at the new Yas Island Marina Circuit in Abu Dhabi. It's a high-profile three-day event; in addition to fast cars and high-octane thrills, the weekend usually includes concert performances by big name entertainers to top off the experience. The event takes place in November; check formula1.com for the dates. The Dubai Autodrome (dubaiautodrome.com) is an FIA-approved circuit that hosts legs of international racing series. The Abu Dhabi Desert Challenge (abudhabidesertchallenge.com), previously known as the UAE Desert Challenge, is another popular event where motorbikes and 4WDs battle it out over the dunes.

Rugby

Emirates Airline Dubai Rugby Sevens

04 321 0008

The Sevens, Al Marmoom

dubairugby7s.com

One of the biggest events in the UAE, the Dubai Rugby Sevens (dubairugby7s.com) attracts a huge crowd each year. The three-day event is the first stop in the IRB Sevens World Series and plays host to the top 16 Sevens teams in the world. The first day of the event sees regional teams go head to head, with the international teams joining the fray for the last two days. As well as the international matches, you can also watch social, youth and women's games at the event. There's a trend for people to attend the event in fancy dress. Tickets can sell out weeks in advance, so plan early.

Tennis

Dubai Duty Free Tennis Championships

04 417 2415

Dubai Tennis Stadium, Al Garhoud

dubaidutyfreetennischampionships.com

The Dubai Tennis Championships takes place every February at The Aviation Club in Garhoud and attracts some of the world's top players. The event is firmly established on the international tennis calendar, and features both men's and ladies' tournaments. Tickets for the later stages sell out in advance so keep an eye out for sale details – entrance to some of the earlier rounds can be bought on the day.

Map 4 D6 **Metro** GGICO

Out Of Dubai

Dubai may offer everything from sun to snow, but there are interesting events held just outside of the emirate should you want to venture further afield.

Abu Dhabi Desert Challenge
02 296 1122

Empty Quarter, Abu Dhabi   abudhabidesertchallenge.com

The Abu Dhabi Desert Challenge is a hot and heavy competition held in the desert around Abu Dhabi. The event sees motorbikes, 4WDs and quad bikes traverse the dunes on a five-day rally. The Desert Challenge takes place in a few different locations, including Moreeb Hill. Check the website for details of the routes – spectators are welcome.

Abu Dhabi HSBC Golf Championship
02 558 8990

Abu Dhabi Golf Club,
 Abu Dhabi   abudhabigolfchampionship.com

With some of the biggest names in golf in attendance, the annual Abu Dhabi Golf Championship is a popular event. The European PGA Tour curtain-raiser is held at the Abu Dhabi Golf Club (02 558 8990, adgolfclub.com) in January; in addition to golf, there's children's entertainment, competitions and an array of food and beverage outlets.

Al Ain Aerobatic Show
800 555

Al Ain Intl Airport, Al Ain   alainaerobaticshow.com

This popular annual event, held every winter at Al Ain Airport, attracts thousands of spectators. The event features some incredible stunt flying with model aircrafts, helicopters, wingwalkers, gliders, and military and civilian planes. There is a festival atmosphere, with tents and displays, and children are well catered for with a play area and bouncy castles. There are a few places to get food, but it may be worth packing a picnic.

Formula 1 Etihad Airways Abu Dhabi Grand Prix
02 659 9999

Yas Marina Circuit, Abu Dhabi — yasmarinacircuit.com

The annual Formula 1 Etihad Airways Abu Dhabi Grand Prix has been a major event on the UAE sporting calendar since 2009. Fans of the sport get to enjoy a close view of the action on the world-class FIA sanctioned, 5.6km Yas Marina Circuit, and concerts by big name performers top off the experience. The race takes place on Yas Island, approximately one hour's drive from Dubai, in November.

Mubadala World Tennis Championship
02 493 8888

Abu Dhabi International Tennis Complex, Zayed Sports City, Abu Dhabi — mubadalawtc.com

Abu Dhabi's first international tennis championship was held in January 2009 and top seeds Roger Federer and Rafael Nadal are among the names to battle it out here. The three-day event features family attractions for spectators, as well as a series of tennis-based activities and tournaments during the run-up to the event, including the Community Cup. Day one sees the elimination round; day two hosts the semis, and day three climaxes with the final and consolation match. The event takes place over New Year's celebrations.

Spas

Take some time out from the city's frenetic pace to enjoy a massage, facial or hammam – you won't have to go far to find one.

A comprehensive range of treatments is on offer in the city and you can find spas offering anything from Balinese massage, hammams and Moroccan baths, to ayurvedic treatments and hot-stone therapy in Dubai's five-star hotels.

The price of treatments varies between spas, and while basic treatments like manicures and pedicures can be cheaper in the smaller spas and salons, you will often pay a high price for more exotic treatments in the upmarket hotels. Lesser known options are just as good and often cheaper. Jumeira has several smaller spas, treatment centres and nail salons that cater for those on a more modest budget and you'll find them inside fancy villas along the beach road and Al Wasl Road.

Spas will often offer set packages that combine a few treatments to make your visit more cost-effective. Compare packages between spas to get the best deal – and ask about their facilities as you will often be allowed to use the sauna, pool or Jacuzzi before or after your treatment.

Some spas only serve women, but others offer treatments for couples in private rooms, or have separate areas for men. Grooming lounges like 1847, which cater exclusively to men, are also increasingly popular.

1847

Grosvenor House, Marsa Dubai

04 399 8989
1847uae.com

Considered the first dedicated 'grooming lounge' for men in the Middle East, 1847 offers manicures, professional shaves and massages in a decidedly manly setting. Several of the treatments take place in private studies, with personal LCD TVs. There is another lounge in The Boulevard at Emirates Towers (04 330 1847) and The Walk at Jumeirah Beach Residence (04 437 0252). **Map** 3 B1 **Metro** DAMAC

Ahasees Spa & Club

Grand Hyatt Dubai, Umm Hurair 2

04 317 2335
dubai.grand.hyatt.com

Although this is a relatively large spa, its atmosphere and attention to detail are spot on. The relaxation area is lit by rows of candles and the wet area (which has a Jacuzzi, plunge pool, steam room and spacious showers) is peppered with rose petals. A broad range of treatments are available, from facials designed to help preserve youthfulness, to massages using essential oils. **Map** 4 B6 **Metro** Healthcare City

Akaru Spa

Jumeirah Creekside Hotel, Al Garhoud

04 230 8565
jumeirah.com

The autumnal colours, natural decor, wooden fittings and glass features create a truly tranquil retreat at this luxurious Garhoud favourite. The menu of exotic treatments on offer range from various specialised facials and wraps, to microdermabrasion.
Map 4 D6 **Metro** GGICO

Amara Spa Dubai

Park Hyatt Dubai, Port Saeed

04 602 1234

dubai.park.hyatt.com

Nestled in stunning surroundings on the banks of the Dubai Creek, Amara Spa is a luxurious treat. The treatment rooms act as your personal spa and, after being treated to one of the fantastic facials or massages, you'll get to enjoy your own private outdoor shower and relaxation area.

Map 4 D5 **Metro** GGICO

Angsana Spa & Health Club Dubai Marina

Al Mamsha St, Marsa Dubai

04 368 4356

angsanaspa.com

Angsana Spa is a haven of Thai-style relaxation in the heart of Marsa Dubai. This is not among the flashy, five-star hotel spas that have come to define the Dubai spa scene in some parts of town; instead, you'll find a tranquil space with impeccable attention to detail and skilled therapists to deliver a soothing massage or beauty treat. Choose from a wide range of treatments – the massages in particular are highly recommended. **Map** 3 B1 **Metro** DAMAC

B/Attitude Spa

Grosvenor House,
Marsa Dubai

04 399 8888

battitudespa-dubai.com

Sister venue to Buddha Bar, this stylish spa oozes oriental chic. Dark colours and soothing DJ tunes set the scene and the treatments range from Eastern massages to Ayurvedic therapies; Swiss Bellefontaine facials are also available.

Map 3 B1 **Metro** DAMAC

The Spa At The Address Downtown Dubai

Cleopatra's Spa & Wellness
04 324 7700
Wafi, Umm Hurair 2   cleopatrasspaandwellness.com

Cleopatra's Spa may not have the grand entrance that some hotel spas share, but what it lacks in ostentation it makes up for in other ways. The relaxation area is an ancient Egypt-esque affair with drapes, silk cushions and *majlis*-style seats. The spa menu features massages and facials, body wraps and anti-ageing treatments. **Map** 4 B5 **Metro** Healthcare City

De La Mer Day Spa
04 328 2775
Jumeira St, Umm Suqeim 2   delamerspa.com

This Jumeira retreat is perfect for a girly get together, with massages, manicures and pedicures on offer. Soak up some sun in the secluded garden, which has a swimming pool and an outdoor Jacuzzi. You can book the VIP suite for special occasions, bringing your own food, drink and decorations. **Map** 1 F2 **Metro** First Gulf Bank

Heavenly Spa By Westin Dubai Mina Seyahi

Westin Dubai Mina Seyahi Beach 04 511 7901
  Resort & Marina, Marsa Dubai westinminaseyahi.com

Similar to other luxury spas in the immediate area, the service here leaves nothing to be desired. The contemporary decor still manages to feel warm and inviting, helping to clear your mind for the gorgeous treatments that await, which includes a fabulous four-handed Heavenly Massage.

Map 3 B1 **Metro** Nakheel

Man/Age

04 437 0868

Arjaan by Rotana, Al Sufouh 1 managespa.com

This luxury men's spa offers all male grooming essentials, with the menu including everything from haircuts and shaving, to manicures, massages and facials. There's also a Moroccan bath for a relaxing treat with local flair.

Map 3 A1 **Metro** DAMAC

Mandara Spa

04 501 8888

The H Hotel Dubai, Trade Center 1 mandaraspa.com

The epicentre of this elegant spa is a circular, cocoon-like chamber containing a grand Jacuzzi pool, and from here you'll find your way to the communal changing room, sauna, steam room and atmospheric treatment rooms. Many of the body therapies on offer start with a foot washing ritual, and the quality of service is evident – nowhere more so than in the four-hands massage which is executed with expert synchronicity.

Map 2 E1 **Metro** World Trade Centre

Akaru Spa

One&Only Private Spa
04 440 1040

One&Only The Palm, Palm Jumeirah,
Nakhlat Jumeira   thepalm.oneandonlyresorts.com

The emphasis in this serene setting is on understated decor, with plenty of neutral colours and natural light. The relaxation room is a haven of tranquillity and an ideal spot to savour the sensations after your treatment. Its speciality is the 'canyon love stone therapy', an energy-balancing massage using warm and cool stones.

Map 3 B1 **Metro** Nakheel

Oriental Hammam
04 315 2140

One&Only Royal Mirage, Al Sufouh 2   oneandonlyresorts.com

This is the ultimate in Arabian luxury. The surroundings are elegant, but not overly opulent, with a warm traditional feel. The hammam and spa is an impressive area with mosaic-covered arches and intricate carvings. The treatment involves being bathed, steamed, and washed with traditional black soap. It may sound invasive, but it is wonderfully invigorating.

Map 3 B1 **Metro** Nakheel

The Ritz-Carlton Spa
04 318 6520

The Ritz-Carlton, Marsa Dubai   ritzcarlton.com

The opulence of the Ritz-Carlton quietly asserts itself amidst the brash, trendy spots that dominate Dubai's beachfront and the hotel's spa is very much in keeping with the resort's general character. With treatments like Ritz's 24 carat gold massage, don't expect bargains here, but sheer delight, yes.

Map 3 A1 **Metro** DAMAC

Mandara Spa

Saray Spa

04 319 4630

Dubai Marriott Harbour Hotel & Suites,
Marsa Dubai

marriott.com

Taking its name from the caravanserais of the ancient Silk
Route, the Saray Spa offers an Arabian-inspired experience.
The spa's signature product range features natural and
traditionally used elements from around the region
including lemon, coffee, mint, frankincense, honey, rose,
pomegranate and dates, as well as Dead Sea salts and mud.
In addition to signature treatments, you could also opt for a
more conventional Swedish massage or try the traditional
hammam experience. However you choose to be pampered,
you will leave feeling relaxed and revived.

Map 3 B1 **Metro** DAMAC

SensAsia Urban Spa

The Village, Jumeira 1

04 349 8850
sensasiaspas.com

SensAsia is one of the most popular spas among Dubai expats and it's not hard to see why. The quality of service is excellent, the therapists well-trained and whichever branch you choose to visit, the treatments delivered in a gorgeous Asian-inspired setting. The emphasis is on Balinese and Thai-style treatments, although Elemis and Eve Lom facials are also available. In addition to the Jumeira venue, branches are located in Palm Jumeirah (04 422 7115) and Emirates Golf Club (04 417 9820)

Map 1 H2 **Metro** Al Jafiliya

Nail Bars

You are never too far from a perfect pedi in Dubai – the city's nail bars are pampering havens where you can enjoy basic treatments and massages in style. You will find at least one nail bar in each of the malls, and popular salons NStyle Nail Lounge (nstyleintl.com) and N.Bar (nbaruae.com) have several locations. Also try The Organic Glow Beauty Lounge (04 380 4666) and Tips & Toes (tipsandtoes.com).

The Spa at Hilton Dubai Jumeirah

04 318 2406
Hilton Dubai Jumeirah Resort, Marsa Dubai
hilton.com

Hilton Jumeirah's spa may not be the most glamorous in town, but the treatments can't be faulted – be it a facial, massage or slimming treatment you're after. The spa also features a relaxation area with a view.

Map 3 A1 **Metro** Jumeirah Lakes Towers

The Spa at Shangri-La

Shangri-La, Trade Center 1

04 405 2441
shangri-la.com

This spa offers a holistic approach to healing, featuring a tempting menu of traditional Asian treatments. The relaxation facilities are extensive, with a salon, barber, juice bar and boutique. Every treatment begins with a welcome drink and foot bath, with therapists pairing holistic spa rituals with the finest European skin care products. Spa treatments are customised to realise personal health and wellness goals. The minimalist surroundings and the communal areas lean more towards fitness club than spa.

Map 2 C1 **Metro** Financial Centre

Spa at The Address Downtown Dubai

The Address Downtown Dubai, Downtown Dubai, Burj Khalifa

04 436 8755

theaddress.com

You step into total relaxation the moment you arrive at this spa, thanks to muted decor, ambient music, and a refreshing drink handed to guests on arrival. Along with an impressive five-tiered pool to dive into, steam rooms, and a rain-dance shower, the Spa has five treatment rooms for women, four for men, a private couple's room, and a range of treatments including facials, massages and wraps using ESPA products. Striking views of Burj Khalifa and The Dubai Fountain complete the experience. The equally inviting spas at The Address Dubai Mall (04 438 8888) and The Address Dubai Marina offer a similarly luxurious experience.

Map 2 B3 **Metro** Burj Khalifa/Dubai Mall

Talise Spa

Burj Al Arab, Umm Suqeim 3

04 301 7338
jumeirah.com

Located in the ultra-exclusive Burj Al Arab, this is as elaborate a spot as you might expect. Bathed in natural light, this luxurious spa offers an extensive menu of pampering treatments, all designed to reinvigorate and restore. From facials and organic body wraps, to Chakra balancing hot stone massages, there is something to tempt everyone. The spa has female-only and mixed environments, including a gym with studios, saunas, steam rooms, plunge pools and two infinity pools looking out over the Arabian Gulf. Relaxation is guaranteed.

Map 3 E1 **Metro** Mall of the Emirates

Talise Spa

Madinat Jumeirah, Al Sufouh 1

04 366 6821
madinatjumeirah.com

This regal spa is made up of luxurious lounges and treatment rooms, connected by garden walkways. You can catch some rays by the charming pool between treatments, complete with loungers, umbrellas, and complimentary bottles of ice cold mineral water and fresh fruit – or you can head inside to enjoy the facilities, which include relaxation areas, an infra-red sauna, steam rooms, and plunge pools. The spa boasts 26 treatment rooms, inclusive of two couples' suites. The focus of the treatments is on natural therapies, with each designed to transform the mind, body and soul. The spa also runs Full Moon Yoga sessions on the beach, with the sound of the waves and close-up views of the Burj Al Arab hotel.

Map 3 E1 **Metro** Mall of the Emirates

Oriental hammam

Shopping

Do Buy   180
Where To Go For...   184
Souks & Markets   190
Shopping Malls   198
Department Stores   212

Do Buy

With souks, boutiques and mammoth malls at every turn, you won't have any problems spending your holiday money in Dubai.

Dubai provides many opportunities to indulge in a shopping spree: it is either a shopaholic's dream or nightmare, depending on who's paying the bill. Dubai's malls are gleaming hubs of trade filled with a mix of international high-street brands and designer names. Most people head to the malls as their first stop, but it is also worth checking out some of Dubai's independent shops.

In the summer, malls are a good place to escape the soaring heat, and with most shops open until at least 10pm every night, and some until midnight at the weekends, there's plenty of time to browse. It takes a dedicated shopper to tackle the malls when they are at their busiest on a Friday evening.

Not content with the large number of existing malls, developers are building even more; a grand mall on Palm Jumeirah is due to open in 2016 and will house 200 shops, a nine-screen cinema and more, and The Beach, a JBR beachfront shopping district with an open-air feel, opened last year with its own 10 screen cinema.

Souks provide an authentic way to shop; they hold a broad range of items, including souvenirs and traditional gifts, and you are able to bargain with traders to get a good price.

Saks Fifth Avenue

While prices for most items are comparable to elsewhere in the world, there are not many places that can beat Dubai's range and frequency of sales.

There are several places to buy carpets and gold jewellery, but you'll need to bargain hard to get a good price. Electronics can be cheaper than they are in the UK or the US, and Dubai is the world's leading re-exporter of gold. For most items, there is enough choice to find something to fit any budget, from the streets of Karama with its fake designer goods, to the shops in the malls that sell the real thing. For the lowdown on where to find your essential Dubai buys, see Where To Go For...

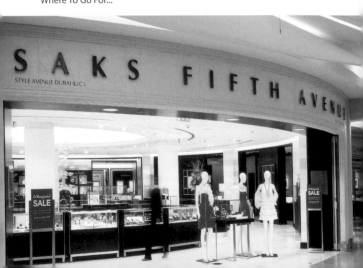

Sizing

Figuring out your size is fairly straightforward. International sizes are often printed on garment labels or the store will usually have a conversion chart on display. Otherwise, a UK size is always four higher than a US size (so a UK 10 is a US 6). To convert European sizes into US sizes, subtract 32 (so a European 38 is actually a US 6). To convert European sizes into UK sizes, a 38 is roughly a 10. As for shoes, a woman's UK 6 is a European 39 or US 8.5 and a men's UK 10 is a European 44 or a US 10.5.

Bargaining

Bargaining is still common practice in the souks and shopping areas of the UAE; you'll need to give it a go to get the best prices. Before you take the plunge, try to get an idea of prices from a few shops, as there can often be a significant difference. Once you've decided how much you are willing to spend, offer an initial bid that is roughly around half that price. Stay laidback and vaguely disinterested. When your initial offer is rejected (and it will be), keep going until you reach an agreement or until you have reached your limit. If the price isn't right, say so and walk out – the vendor will often follow and suggest a compromise price. The more you buy, the better the discount. When the price is agreed, it is considered bad form to back out of the sale.

While common in souks, bargaining isn't commonly accepted in malls and independent shops. However, use your discretion, as some shops such as jewellery stores, smaller electronics stores and eyewear optical centres do operate a set discount system and the price shown may be 'before discount'. Ask whether there is a discount on the marked price and you may end up with a bargain.

Shipping

The large number of international and local shipping and courier agencies makes transporting anything from a coffee pot to a car feasible. Both air and sea freight are available; air freight is faster but more expensive and not really suitable for large or heavy objects, whereas sea freight may take several weeks to arrive but it is cheaper and, as it is possible to rent containers, size and weight are not as much of an issue. With so many companies to choose from, it is worth getting a few quotes and finding out what will happen when the goods arrive; some offer no services at the destination while others, usually the bigger ones, will clear customs and deliver right to the door. For smaller items, or those that have to be delivered quickly, air freight is better, and the items can be tracked. Empost (600 56 5555) offers both local and international courier and air freight services at competitive prices.

Mall Eats

Dubai has some fantastic cafes and restaurants in its malls. The Lime Tree Cafe & Kitchen at Ibn Battuta Mall, Aprés and Almaz by Momo at Mall of the Emirates, The Cheesecake Factory (04 325 3521) at The Dubai Mall and Shake Shack (04 315 3612) at Mercato Mall should get you ready for more retail therapy.

Art

The art scene in Dubai, quiet for so long, has been enjoying rapid growth over the past few years. There are galleries and exhibitions displaying traditional and contemporary art by Arabic and international artists working in a range of media. The Majlis Gallery (04 353 6233, themajlisgallery.com), located in a traditional windtower house, is a great venue for fine art, hand-made glass, pottery and other unusual pieces. For cutting edge art, check out Opera Gallery (04 323 0909, operagallery.com) or XVA Gallery (04 353 5383, xvagallery.com), while Art Source (04 285 6972, artsource-llc.com) in Rashidiya stocks a range of original artwork – a framing service is also offered. You can find information on art auctions, as well as art fairs and gallery openings at artinthecity.com.

Souk Madinat Jumeirah has the largest concentration of boutiques selling art, glass and photographs, both originals and reproductions. Many of the galleries and showrooms have a framing service or can recommend one. There are some excellent framing shops on Plant Street in Satwa (Map 1 N4) and in Karama Market (Map 5 A4).

An Arabian Shopping Experience

There are a few places in Dubai where you can sidestep the glitzy mall experience and enjoy more authentic Arabian-style shopping. The bohemian Al Fahidi Historical Neighbourhood, formerly known as Bastakiya, has narrow walkways, traditional windtowers and courtyards, which provide the perfect setting for artisans to sell their wares.

Souk Madinat Jumeirah's winding walkways are a great place to shop for jewellery, photography and art, while Souk Al Bahar has some quirky boutiques and furniture stores selling traditional items. Wafi's underground marketplace, Khan Murjan, houses 150 stalls underneath its spectacular stained glass ceiling. Trade Routes, inside Dubai Festival City, is another modern take on traditional Arabian souks. Each area holds a broad range of shops as well as several restaurants should you need to refuel.

Carpets

Carpets are one of the region's signature items, although they tend to be imported from Iran, Turkey and Pakistan. The price of a piece depends on a number of factors: its origin, the material used, the number of knots, and whether or not it is hand-made. The

Fake Goods

The consumer protection department of the Dubai Department of Economic Development (dubaided. gov.ae) previously had a crackdown on the sale of counterfeit goods; however, the sale of such items is still very common in Dubai. If it has a logo, then you'll be able to find a 'genuine copy' version of it in Karama. The quality of goods varies, with some items being almost indistinguishable from the originals, and others being hilariously bad imitations. You'll want to inspect items properly to ensure you are buying the genuine article and not a very good fake.

most expensive carpets are usually those hand-made with silk in Iran. The higher the quality, the neater the back, so turn the carpets over – if the pattern is clearly depicted and the knots are all neat, the carpet is of higher quality than those that are indistinct. Try to do some research so that you have a basic idea of what you are looking for before you go, just in case you happen to meet an unscrupulous carpet dealer. Fortunately, most will happily explain the differences between the rugs and share their extensive knowledge.

Ask to see a selection of various carpets and get a feel for the differences between hand-made or machine-made silk, wool or blend carpets. Expect prices to range from a few hundred to tens of thousands of dirhams. It is always worth bargaining to get a better price. To find the perfect piece, head to Fabindia (Al Mankhool St, Bur Dubai, 04 398 9633), the Pride of Kashmir (04 368 6110) in Souk Madinat Jumeirah and Mercato Mall, or Persian Carpet House (04 330 3277) in the Emirates Towers. There's also a good collection of places in Deira, among them National Iranian Carpets (04 368 6002).

Gold

Gold is notably cheaper in the UAE than in Europe, making it a popular souvenir and a main attraction for many visitors. Dubai is the world's leading re-exporter of gold and you'll find a jeweller in even the smallest of malls. It is available in 18, 21, 22 and 24 carats and is sold according to the international gold rate. This means that, for an identical piece, whether you buy it in Mall of the Emirates or in the Gold Souk, there should be very little difference in price. You should do your research before buying anything though, especially if you decide to get a piece custom-made to a design, such as a necklace with your name in Arabic. Of course, don't forget to bargain.

Many of the world's finest jewellery stores have outlets in Dubai. Both Cartier and Tiffany have numerous branches throughout the city. Simply asking for a discount, even in these upmarket retailers, can get good results. You'll find a large selection of outlets, most of which are open to bargaining, in the Gold & Diamond Park (04 362 7777) at Interchange 4 on Sheikh Zayed Road, and this venue offers a slightly cooler, less frenetic shopping experience than the Gold Souk.

Souvenirs

There is the usual selection of tacky souvenirs available in Dubai, but an equally impressive range of tasteful items are much more worthy of your money. Hand-carved wooden trinket boxes, sometimes filled with traditional *oudh* (a kind of incense) are popular, as are beaded wall hangings from the Textile Souk, *khanjars* (traditional Arabic daggers), pashminas and *keffiyeh* headscarves, embroidered slippers, hand-woven carpets and shisha pipes. For the ultimate in Arabian kitsch, pick up a gaudy mosque alarm clock that wakes you up with the sound of the call to prayer – it won't win you any style awards, but you'll probably be the only person on your street that has one. Good places to hunt for souvenirs include Souk Madinat Jumeirah and Karama.

Tailoring

If you happen to be staying in town for longer than a few days, it is a great opportunity to get some garments made. Tailors can be found in most areas, but the area around Dubai Museum in Al Souk Al Kabeer, or Plant Street in Satwa, are good places to start. A good tailor will be able to make a garment from scratch (rather than just make alterations), either from a photo or diagram, or by copying an existing item. If they don't get the garment spot on, they will happily make the necessary alterations. Allow one week or more to make sure you don't run out of time for alterations after the first fitting.

Dream Girl Tailors (04 349 5445) in Satwa has a huge following: it is great for everything from taking up trousers to making ball gowns. Skirts here cost around Dhs.60 and dresses from around Dhs.150, depending on the complexity of the pattern. Dream Boy (04 352 1840), in Meena Bazaar, is good for shirts and suits, as is Whistle and Flute (04 342 9229); shirts usually start from Dhs.85 and suits from around Dhs.1,000. One of Dubai's most highly regarded tailors is Kachins (04 352 1386), where you may pay a little extra for a suit or shirt, but the fabric and cut will be worth it. Santoba Tailors (04 393 1234), near Choithram in Meena Bazaar, is another great option. Its tailors will design, copy, or alter suits, dresses and anything else you can think up – it specialises in European designs and slick shirts and suits.

Clockwise from top left: Al Fahidi Street, Karama Market, 2nd December Street

Souks & Markets

If you want to add a slice of cultural indulgence to your shopping list, head to the souks where you'll find bargains amid the bustle.

There are a number of souks and markets in Dubai. The souks are the traditional trading areas, some more formally demarcated than others. In keeping with tradition, bargaining is expected and cash gives the best leverage.

The Gold, Spice and Textile Souks line either side of the creek, but parking is limited, so if possible it is better to go to these areas by taxi or, if you are visiting all three, park on one side of the creek and take an abra to the other side.

Western-style markets are becoming more popular: they are usually based around crafts and are often seasonal. Marina Market is set up along Marina Walk during the cooler months. Ripe Market in Zabeel Park on Friday mornings throughout winter, offers up local organic produce and crafty items, ideal as gifts. Both are great launch pads for local talents, with artists and jewellers displaying their wares.

Global Village (globalvillage.ae), on Sheikh Mohammed bin Zayed Road near Arabian Ranches (Map 1 E9), is a huge collection of stalls, food and entertainment from all over the world. It runs from October to March every day of the week, and is a good spot to pick up everything from Chinese lanterns to honey from Yemen. Organised by country, you can spend hours exploring the wares before enjoying a unique range of dishes in the international foodcourt. Just don't overdo dinner before getting on the fairground rides. Global Village is open from 4pm to midnight, Saturday to Wednesday, and until 1am on Thursday and Friday. Entrance costs Dhs.10 and is free for children under three years old.

Marina Market

The promenade behind Dubai Marina Mall is the new home for this cute little market, which is packed full of funky clothes, accessories, souvenirs, home decor items and children's products. Having moved along Marina Walk from the far end, the new location means that the mall cafes provide a pit stop, and views across the marina make for a pleasant backdrop. The market runs every Wednesday from 10am to 10pm, and every Thursday to Saturday from 10am until 11pm, and there's parking at Marina Mall.
Map 3 A1 **Metro** Jumeirah Lake Towers

Dubai Flea Market

This flea market is a great place to take advantage of Dubai's transient population, who gather to sell their belongings before leaving Dubai. As people pack up and move on, an escapee's excess baggage could become a bargain hunter's treasure. For the Dhs.5 entry fee into Zabeel Park, or the market at Uptown Mirdif, you can peruse the stalls covered with furniture, books, clothing and a broad range of unwanted items and home-made crafts. See the Dubai Flea Market website (dubai-fleamarket.com) for dates. It's also held at JLT and Ibn Battuta. Another market, the Dubai Designer

Market (dubaidesignermarket.com), takes place on the second Saturday of every month in the Beach Centre, Jumeira Road. It's free to enter and you'll find genuine second-hand luxury goods – check the website for the schedule.
Map 1 G2 **Metro** Business Bay

Electronics Souk

At the heart of Bur Dubai's traditional shopping area, and bordering the Textile Souk, Al Fahidi Street is home to Dubai's Electronics Souk. A great place to wander round in the cooler evenings, it's perfect for a bit of local colour and some great shopping. This area is always busy but it really comes to life at night – if you're unsure whether you're in the right place, just head for the neon lights. Prices are negotiable and competitive but the vendors know the value of what they're selling. Don't make your purchases at the first shop you go into; rather, take the time to look around at the range and prices available. Although goods are often cheaper here, if you are making a big purchase, it may be worth paying that bit extra at a major retailer, so that you have more security if something goes wrong. **Map** 4 C2 **Metro** Al Ghubaiba

Gold Souk

This is Dubai's best-known souk and a must-do for every visitor. In addition to being an exotic experience to remember, the souk is a good place to buy customised jewellery for unique souvenirs and gifts at a reasonable price.

On the Deira side of the creek, the meandering lanes are lined with shops selling gold, silver, pearls and precious stones. These can be bought as they are, or in a variety of settings so this is definitely a place to try your bargaining skills – let the vendor offer you the best discount to get the ball rolling. Gold is sold by weight according to the daily international price and so will be much the same as in the shops in malls – the price of the workmanship is where you will have more bargaining power. Most of the outlets operate split shifts, so try not to visit between 1pm and 4pm as many will be closed. The Gold Souk is shaded so visiting during the hotter daytime hours is an option, but there is added sparkle when you visit in the evenings as the lights reflect on the gold and gems. **Map** 4 C2 **Metro** Al Ras

Karama Complex

Karama is one of the older residential districts in Dubai, and it has a big shopping area that is one of the best places to find a bargain. The best spot is the Karama Complex (also known as Karama Market), a long street running through the middle of the district that is lined by shops on both sides. The area is best known for bargain clothing, sports goods, gifts and souvenirs, and it is notorious for being the hotbed of counterfeit items in Dubai. As you wander round, you will be offered 'copy watches, copy bags', and if you show any interest you will be whisked into a back room to view the goods. If you're not interested, a simple 'no thank you' will suffice, or even just ignore the vendor completely – it may seem rude, but sometimes it's the only way to cope with the incessant invitations to view counterfeit items. Two of the most popular shops are Blue Marine and Green Eye, while the imaginatively named Asda is around the corner, and offers high-quality handbags and accessories crammed into two floors. It's pretty claustrophobic but the range is excellent.

There's a huge range of T-shirts, shoes, shorts and sunglasses at very reasonable prices in Karama. There are several shops selling gifts and souvenirs, from toy camels to mosque alarm clocks and stuffed scorpions to pashminas. Gifts Tent (04 335 4416) is one of the larger outlets and has a wide range, including every colour of pashmina imaginable. The salesmen are happy to take most of them out so you can find exactly the right shade. With loads of small, inexpensive restaurants serving a range of cuisines, you won't go hungry while pounding the streets of Karama. Try Chef Lanka (04 335 3050), Aryaas (04 335 5776) or Saravana Bhavan.
Map 4 B3 **Metro** ADCB

Khan Murjan

For something a little different, head to Wafi's underground souk. Khan Murjan's magnificent stained glass ceiling (which stretches 64m) and long curved arches help make this an atmospheric place to shop. The souk features over 150 stalls selling jewellery, antiques, Arabic perfumes and souvenirs. It is particularly good if you wish to spice up your home with traditional arts and crafts; there are workshops where artisans can create various bits of arts and crafts on site. In the centre of the souk, you'll find an open air marble courtyard and the Khan Murjan Restaurant (04 327 9795), which serves tasty pan-Arabic culinary treats.
Map 4 B5 **Metro** Healthcare City

Souk Al Bahar

While this isn't a souk in the conventional sense, Souk Al Bahar, in Downtown Dubai, is a modern take on the concept: similar to the souk at Madinat Jumeirah, the Arabian-style mall features dimly lit corridors, carved wood and a small range of shops. Compared to the retail extravaganza of the adjacent Dubai Mall, Souk Al Bahar is unlikely to set a serious shopper's pulse racing but the atmospheric setting makes for a fun experience – not to mention excellent photo opportunities. It's also a good spot to stock up on souvenirs. Stop by at Fortix (04 420 3680) for small gifts to bring home, or try Pride of Kashmir (04 420 3606) to bag an exotic rug. For unique household items, Marina Exotic Home Interiors (04 420 0191) carries a range of home decoration pieces with a distinct regional flair.

The main reason for turning up at Souk Al Bahar is the centre's vibrant bar and dining scene. Thai restaurant, Mango Tree (04 426 7313), has great food and superb fountain views, while Claw (04 432 2300) offers ribs, lobsters, crabs and steaks. Once darkness falls, there are several bars for a post-shop cool down and refuelling opportunity.

Map 2 B3 **Metro** Burj Khalifa/Dubai Mall

Souk Madinat Jumeirah

Souk Madinat Jumeirah is a recreation of a traditional souk, complete with narrow alleyways, authentic architecture and motorised abras. The blend of outlets is unlike anywhere else in Dubai, with boutique shops, galleries, cafes, restaurants and bars. The layout can be a little confusing; there are maps throughout and the main features are signposted. If you're really lost, staff will happily direct you. The souk is home to a concentration of art boutiques, including Gallery One which sells photos with a local flavour (04 368 6055) and Spirit of Art Gallery (04 368 6207). The stalls in the outside areas sell souvenirs, some tasteful and some tacky. For holiday clobber, eye-catching but expensive swimming gear can be found at Vilebrequin (04 368 6531), Via Rodeo (04 368 6568) and Tommy Bahama (04 368 6031).

There are more than 20 waterfront cafes, bars and restaurants to choose from, including some of Dubai's hottest night spots: Trader Vic's and Barzar are among the popular choices around here, to name a few. There's also the impressive Madinat Theatre (madinattheatre.com) which sees international and regional artists perform everything from ballet to comedy.

Map 3 E1 **Metro** Mall of the Emirates

Spice Souk

With its narrow streets and exotic aromas, a wander through the Spice Souk, next to the Gold Souk, is a great way to get a feel for the way the city used to be. Most of the stalls sell the same ranges and the vendors are usually happy to advise on the types of spices and their uses. This is a good spot to pick up an exotic souvenir or two – you may even be able to pick up some saffron at a bargain price. The shops operate split shifts, but there is more bustle in the evenings. Friday is not the best day to visit as many of the shops are closed until the evening. **Map** 4 C2 **Metro** Al Ras

Textile Souk

Textile Souk

The Textile Souk in Al Souk Al Kabeer is stocked with every fabric and colour imaginable. Textiles are imported from all over the world, with many of the more elaborate coming from the Indian subcontinent and the Far East. There are silks and satins in an amazing array of colours and patterns, velvets and intricately embroidered fabrics. Basic cottons can sometimes be harder to find but you can always try Satwa. Prices are negotiable and there are often sales, particularly around the major holidays of Eid and Diwali, and the shopping festivals. It is worth having a look in a few shops before parting with your cash as stock and prices vary considerably. The mornings tend to be a more relaxed time to browse.

Nearby, Meena Bazaar is the area that most taxi drivers head for if you ask for the Textile Souk. It has an impressive number of fabric stores. Rivoli Textiles (04 335 0075) has a good selection. Be sure to haggle. **Map** 4 C2 **Metro** Al Ghubaiba

Shopping Malls

More than merely shopping destinations, Dubai's malls are epicentres of activity, with eating, drinking and even skiing on offer.

BurJuman

04 352 0222
burjuman.com

Shk Khalifa Bin Zayed St, Al Mankhool

One of Dubai's original shopping havens, BurJuman is renowned for its blend of designer and high-street labels attracting many a well-heeled shopper. The mall houses many famous brands, including Christian Dior, Gap, Escada and Just Cavalli, as well as some interesting smaller shops and legendary New York department store Saks Fifth Avenue. In addition to clothing and fashion, you can stock up on electronics, home decor and sports goods. There are also a few independent music shops that sell a good range of CDs and DVDs, and a branch of Virgin Megastore. The two foodcourts and numerous cafes are well arranged for people-watching, including the popular Pavilion Gardens on the third floor, and Paul on the ground floor, where you can dine outside during the cooler months. The mall can be accessed directly from Dubai Metro and there is plenty of underground parking and a taxi rank just outside (this gets pretty congested after 6pm and at weekends). Major renovation and expansion works have recently been completed and there is now also a branch of Carrefour supermarket.

Map 4 B3 **Metro** BurJuman

BurJuman

Deira City Centre

04 295 1010
Al Ittihad St, Port Saeed
deiracitycentre.com

A stalwart of Dubai's mall scene, this centre attracts the most cosmopolitan crowd. The three floors offer a diverse range of shops where you can find anything from a postcard to a Persian carpet. There's an 11 screen cinema, a children's entertainment centre, a jewellery court, a bowling alley, a textiles court and an area dedicated to local furniture, gifts and souvenirs.

It's all anchored by a huge Carrefour hypermarket, Paris Gallery and Debenhams. In addition, many high-street brands are represented, including Gap, Warehouse, Topshop, Forever 21, Next and River Island. A number of designer boutiques can be found, mostly on the top floor. The City Gate section (on the same level as car parks P2 and P3) is dominated by electronics retailers.

The mall has two foodcourts: one on the first floor, next to Magic Planet, serving mainly fast food, and one on the second floor, featuring several good sit-down restaurants. Thanks to the Deira City Centre Metro station, it is now easier to get to and from than before – which is great because the taxi queues can get very long, especially during weekends and in the evenings. **Map** 4 D5 **Metro** Deira City Centre

Dubai Festival City

800 332
Crescent Dr, Al Kheeran
festivalcentre.com

Dubai Festival City incorporates the Festival Mall and The Festival Waterfront Centre. The area features around 370 retail outlets (including 25 flagship stores) and more than 90 restaurants, including 40 alfresco dining options. The need for retail therapy can be sated by the broad range of fashion, electronics and homeware outlets spread over 2.9 million square feet of retail space. Brit favourite Marks & Spencer (04 206 6466) is among the big draws here, in addition to numerous high-street clothing labels. For the finer things in life, there is also a 25,000 square foot modern gold souk where you can peruse gold from all over the world.

It's not just shopping though; The Festival Waterfront Centre has dramatic water features and performance spaces to keep shoppers entertained. There is also a Novo Cinemas (04 232 8328) and a 10 lane bowling alley on site. You can happily spend an entire day here, dining at Romano's Macaroni Grill (04 232 6001) before relaxing in the Belgian Beer Cafe. **Map** 1 J4 **Metro** Emirates

Dubai Marina Mall   04 436 1020
Al Marsa St, Marsa Dubai   dubaimarinamall.com
Located in Marsa Dubai's thriving community, and within walking distance of the popular beachfront promenade in Jumeirah Beach Residence, this mall's 160 outlets offer a mix of plush designer goods and high-street regulars. Shops like New Look (04 399 7740), Reiss (04 399 7664), Karen Millen (04 399 7525), Ted Baker (04 399 7377) and Accessorize (04 399 7953) anchor the mall's offering of reasonably priced fashion. You can also pick up kids' items at Mamas and Papas (04 399 7807) or the Early Learning Centre (04 434 2642). If you get hungry while browsing, there are several restaurants and cafes. The large top-floor foodcourt features many of the

usual fast food suspects. On the ground floor and mezzanine level, you'll find more varied options, with restaurants such as Carluccio's (04 399 7844), Gourmet Burger Kitchen (04 399 7705) and Yo! Sushi (04 399 7708) among the popular draws. Many of these restaurants also boast attractive alfresco areas along the water's edge. The Favourite Things play area (04 434 1984, favouritethings.com) provides plenty of entertainment for kids, and you can leave your kids there so they can enjoy supervised play while you shop. There is also a branch of Reel Cinemas (reelcinemas.ae) showing a selection of the latest releases. There's also the seven-storey, licensed Pier 7, offering world-class cuisine with waterfront views.

Map 3 A1 **Metro** Jumeirah Lakes Towers

The Dubai Mall
800 38224 6255

Financial Centre St,
Downtown Dubai, Burj Khalifa   thedubaimall.com

The Dubai Mall is one of the world's largest malls with more than 1,200 stores, including 160 eateries. The huge shopping and entertainment complex houses an extensive range of stores, an Olympic size ice skating rink, a catwalk for fashion shows, an enormous aquarium, a 22 screen cinema, an indoor theme park called SEGA Republic (04 448 8484), a luxury hotel, and a children's edutainment centre called KidZania (kidzania.ae).

The shopping highlights are manifold, but unique to The Dubai Mall are the regional flagship stores for New York department store Bloomingdale's, French department store Galeries Lafayette (04 339 9933), the world-renowned

Welcome to an unforgettable aquatic experience!

Find yourself surrounded by tens of thousands of aquatic animals, experience walking on water from the top of the Aquarium viewing panel, visit the Underwater Zoo on Level 2 and see our Rainforest animals and Creepy Crawlies or take a dive amongst the sharks. It's all part of an aquatic adventure you'll never forget.

Ground & Level 2, The Dubai Mall
Call: +971 4 448 5200 or visit www.thedubaiaquarium.com

Follow "Dubai Aquarium" on f t

DUBAI
AQUARIUM
& UNDERWATER ZOO

toy shop Hamleys (04 339 8889) and UK upmarket food retailer Waitrose (04 434 0700). You'll find all of the haute couture designer brands along Fashion Avenue and there is a sprawling souk with 66 jewellery outlets. Inside the mall, touch-screen maps and knowledgeable staff make it easy to find what you are looking for. For a complete contrast, cross the wooden bridge over the Burj Khalifa Lake and you'll find yourself in Souk Al Bahar. The tranquillity of its dimly lit passageways offers a more relaxing stop after the onslaught of the mall.

Map 2 C3 **Metro** Burj Khalifa/Dubai Mall

Dubai Outlet Mall

04 423 4666

Dubai – Al Ain Rd (Route 66),
Umm Nahad 1   dubaioutletmall.com

In a city where the emphasis is on excess, it is refreshing to find a mall dedicated to saving money. Dubai's first 'outlet' mall may be quite a way out of town, along the Al Ain highway, but bargain hunters will find it's worth the drive. A wide range of luxury brands and designer labels are on offer at heavily discounted prices, in addition to a good selection of bargain sports goods and children's wear. **Map** 1 G7

Ibn Battuta Mall

04 362 1900

Shk Zayed Rd, Jabal Ali   ibnbattutamall.com

This mall is divided into six zones each based on a region that explorer Ibn Battuta visited in the 14th century. There are several anchor stores, including Debenhams and Geant hypermarket (04 368 5880). Shops are loosely grouped: China

Court is dedicated to entertainment, with several restaurants and a 21 screen cinema, including the UAE's first IMAX screen. Nearby is Sharaf DG (04 368 5115), and iStyle (04 366 9797) for fans of Apple products; it also does repairs in case you dropped your iPod into the hotel pool.

The fashion conscious should head to India Court for the likes of Forever 21 (04 368 5232), H&M (04 364 9819), River Island (04 368 5961), Topshop (04 368 5948) and popular independent boutique Ginger & Lace (04 368 5109). Persia Court is designed as the lifestyle area, anchored by Debenhams (04 368 5282). The foodcourts are at either end of the mall. To reward the kids for trailing round after you, there's a Fun City in Tunisia Court. The taxi points are by the entrance to each court. **Map** 1 B2 **Metro** Ibn Battuta Mall

Mall of the Emirates
04 409 9000

Sheikh Zayed Rd, Al Barsha 1   malloftheemirates.com

Mall of the Emirates (MoE) is more than a mall, it's a lifestyle destination. It houses an indoor ski slope (Ski Dubai), the Kempinski hotel, the Sheraton hotel and the Dubai Community Theatre & Arts Centre. There are more than 500 outlets selling everything from forks to high fashion. The mall has been extended to include the Fashion Dome which features a selection of restaurants and fashion outlets including a branch of MORE Cafe (04 395 0967), a Boutique 1 store and Sephora – there are also plenty of designer names. The mall is anchored by a Carrefour hypermarket, Dubai's largest branch of Debenhams, Harvey Nichols and Centrepoint, which is home to Babyshop, Home Centre,

Lifestyle, Shoe Mart and Splash. There is also a VOX Cinemas (04 341 4222) where you can enjoy a film in Gold Class, which means enormous leather armchairs and waiter service throughout. Nearby, the sizeable Magic Planet (04 341 4444) includes a bowling alley, and a myriad of games and rides. Label devotees should head for Rodeo Drive (04 340 0347) to get their fix of designer labels such as Burberry, Dolce & Gabanna, Salvatore Ferragamo, Tod's and Versace. If you're more into high-street chic, there are two H&M stores, a branch of Reiss (04 341 0515), and a large Zara (04 341 3171). Those looking for accessories and jewellery will love Boom & Mellow (04 341 3993). Sporty types should head straight to GO Sport (04 341 3251) for all-season apparel. For entertainment, Virgin Megastore (04 341 4353) has a bookshop and many international magazines alongside CDs, DVDs, mobile phones and computers.

You'll need to keep your energy up to explore this large mall so it's fortunate there is a wide range of dining options, from the Swiss chalet feel of Apres to a large selection of cafes and two foodcourts. Several taxis queue up outside and you can also access the metro directly from the mall.
Map 3 E2 **Metro** Mall of the Emirates

Mercato
04 344 4161
Jumeira St, Jumeira 1   mercatoshoppingmall.com
Mercato is the largest mall in Jumeira, with more than 90 shops, restaurants, cafes and a cinema. As you drive along Jumeira Road, the renaissance-style architecture really makes Mercato stand out, and, once inside, the huge glass roof

provides natural light and enhances the Mediterranean feel. The mall is anchored by a large Spinneys supermarket (04 349 6900), a Virgin Megastore (04 344 6971) and Gap (04 342 0745). There are designer boutiques and high-street brands, and shops range from the reasonably priced Pull and Bear (04 344 7214) to the more exclusive Reiss (04 345 5010). For everyday fashions and holiday essentials, try Topshop (04 344 2677), Massimo Dutti (04 344 7124) and Mango (04 344 7184). A stylish taste of heritage Britain is to be found in the threads sold in Jack Wills (04 419 0082).

There is a foodcourt and a number of cafes and restaurants, including French cafe Paul (04 349 9115) and the popular Shake Shack (04 315 3612). The cinema and large Fun City play area (04 349 9976) should keep most of the family occupied. **Map** 1 G2 **Metro** Financial Centre

Mirdif City Centre
04 602 3000

Shk Mohd Bin Zayed Rd, Mirdif

mirdifcitycentre.com

What makes this mall stand out from the rest? Its bright, modern interior, its mix of high-street and designer brands, and a good few stores that don't have presence elsewhere in Dubai. The mall's highlights include large branches of Boutique 1, Debenhams, Carrefour and Topshop, as well as Dubai debutants Pottery Barn and American Eagle Outfitters. If you have kids in tow, Playnation (playnationme.com) is an emporium of fun times with highlights that include an indoor skydiving centre, a water-themed play centre, a 10 pin bowling alley, an edutainment centre and an arcade. Top it off with a large car park and well-stocked foodcourts, and this is

definitely worth a visit if you're near Mirdif or are staying with friends or relatives based in this part of town.
Map 1 K5 **Metro** Rashidiya

The Walk At Jumeirah Beach Residence 04 390 0091
Jumeirah Beach Residence, Marsa Dubai
While this isn't strictly a mall, and the selection is rather limited, The Walk is great for browsing and cafe culture. It is a fully pedestrianised shopping area that stretches 1.7km along the beachfront. Outlets are either on the ground level or on the plaza level of six clusters of towers called Murjan, Sadaf, Bahar, Rimal, Amwaj and Shams. The plaza level of each cluster can be accessed by stairs or lifts at ground level and in the car park. The largest cluster of shops is concentrated at the Murjan end of the strip. Fashion favourite Boutique 1 (04 425 7888) is here. The Style Outlet carries discounted designer clothing – to the delight of fashion-conscious bargain hunters.

In the afternoons, people congregate in the many cafes in the area – particularly popular are Le Pain Quotidien (04 437 0141) and Paul (04 437 6494), and there are also plenty of alfresco restaurants to dine in. Parking is available along the beach near Bahar, or in the designated visitors area of the Murjan car park. Most of the shops open at 10am and close at 10pm. The new beachfront mall here, known as The Beach, opened in 2014, with more than 70 retail, food, drink and entertainment venues including a 10 screen cinema, as well as a large car park.
Map 3 A1 **Metro** DAMAC

Wafi

04 324 4555
wafi.com

Oud Metha Rd, Umm Hurair 2

Wafi is one of Dubai's most exclusive malls and a popular stop for the Big Bus Tours. The store directory reads like a who's who in design, with a wide range of international labels available to splurge on should you have some holiday cash burning a hole in your pocket. Among some of the mall's most interesting boutiques is Ginger & Lace (04 324 5699) which stocks a mix of funky fashion styles. Alternatively, you could head out to the top-end department store Salam (04 704 8349) to quench your thirst for all manner of designer gear under one roof. For a break from the upper echelons of fashion, there's also a large Marks & Spencer (04 324 5145), offering tried and tested high-street styles and clothing staples from the UK.

The stunning Khan Murjan souk houses over 150 shops selling antiques, jewellery and souvenirs in an atmospheric setting. Shopping aside, there are a number of cafes and restaurants in the mall, including Italian restaurant Biella (04 324 4666), where you can eat in the alfresco dining area. Wafi Gourmet (04 324 4433) is a great place to pick up freshly made Arabic dishes and a delicious selection of olives and dates.

The children's entertainment area, Kids Connection (04 327 9011), has swings, slides, see-saws, springs and trampolines. If you feel the need for pampering, or an evening out, head across to the Pyramids complex where there are some excellent bars and restaurants and a renowned spa.

Map 4 B5 **Metro** Healthcare City

Wafi

Department Stores

The scope of department stores covers the full shopping spectrum, from the epitome of chic at Saks Fifth Avenue to the functionality of M&S.

Debenhams

04 340 7575
debenhams.com

Mall of the Emirates, Al Barsha 1

A stalwart of the British high street, Debenhams has five stores in Dubai: Deira City Centre, Ibn Battuta Mall, Mall of the Emirates, Mirdif City Centre and The Dubai Mall. The branches all stock perfumes and cosmetics, clothing and homewares. They carry the popular Designers at Debenhams range with diffusion lines from John Rocha, Betty Jackson, Jasper Conran, Matthew Williamson and Ben de Lisi.
Map 3 E2 **Metro** Mall of the Emirates

Harvey Nichols

04 409 8888
harveynichols.com

Mall of the Emirates, Al Barsha 1

Dubai simply couldn't call itself a luxury destination without its own Harvey Nichols (the largest branch outside the UK). It contains a large selection of high-rolling fashion, food, beauty and homeware brands, as well as an intimidating selection of sunglasses. Pick up fashion treats from Jimmy Choo, Diane Von Furstenberg, Juicy Couture, Hermes and Sergio Rossi, then head to the top floor for the popular Almaz by Momo (04 409 8877), a restaurant, juice bar and shisha cafe all in one.
Map 3 E2 **Metro** Mall of the Emirates

Bloomingdales

04 350 5333

The Dubai Mall,
  Downtown Dubai, Burj Khalifa   bloomingdales.com
This famous upscale department store houses merchandise
for the home as well as fashion items. There are two locations
– one over three levels selling clothing and accessories,
and another single-level, home store. Staff can provide
personalised assistance, and when the shopping is done you
can treat yourself to a cupcake at the Magnolia Bakery.
Map 2 C3 **Metro** Dubai Mall

Jashanmal

04 232 9023

Dubai Festival City Mall, Al Kheeran   jashanmalgroup.com
One of Dubai's original department stores, Jashanmal is the
importer for several brands including Burberry, Clarks shoes
and Mexx. With books, cameras, fashion, gifts, homeware,
kitchen appliances and luggage on offer, the stores are
definitely worth a look. The new Festival City concept store
also houses a 'Cook and Coffee' lifestyle section, where
cooking demonstrations will take place, and the other
branches are set to follow suit. **Map** 1 J4 **Metro** Emirates

Marks & Spencer

04 206 6466

Dubai Festival City Mall, Al Kheeran marksandspencerme.com
One of the best-known brands in the UK, M&S sells men's,
women's and children's clothes and shoes, along with a small
selection of food. It is famous for its underwear selection
and has a reputation for quality. You'll also find more
fashion-forward lines including Limited Collection, Per Una,

and Autograph alongside the traditional styles it has been carrying for years. The brand new flagship store is located in Mall of the Emirates, while other branches are located in Wafi, Deira City Centre and The Dubai Mall.
Map 1 J4 **Metro** Emirates

Saks Fifth Avenue
04 501 2700
BurJuman, Al Mankhool
saksfifthavenue.com
Anchoring the extension to BurJuman is the second-largest Saks Fifth Avenue outside the US. The stylish store for the label conscious is spread over two floors of paradise. You'll find designers galore, including Christian Dior, Jean Paul Gaultier, Prada, Agent Provocateur and Tiffany & Co, in addition to a personalised shopping service.
Map 4 B3 **Metro** BurJuman

Supermarkets & Hypermarkets

The city's large supermarkets and hypermarkets stock a good range of international products and a comprehensive range of electronics, household goods, luggage and mobile phones. Carrefour (carrefouruae.com) has several locations in the city, and it is the best place to buy French products (particularly good are its crusty bread and selection of French cheeses). Its stores also stock camping gear, clothes, music, DVDs and stationery. Upmarket UK store Waitrose has branches in Dubai Marina Mall (04 434 2624) and The Dubai Mall (04 434 0700) and its deli counter is great for picnic items and snacks. Spinneys (spinneys-dubai.com) stocks a great range of imported food items (including those from Waitrose).

Ibn Battuta Mall

Independent & Noteworthy Shops

Dubai's independent scene has improved greatly in recent years. You'll find the odd store in Souk Al Bahar or The Walk At Jumeirah Beach Residence, but Jumeira Road in Jumeira is one of the most popular destinations; in addition to individual stores in converted villas, the local malls here are fruitful grounds to hunt for unique items and hard-to-find brands.

Fabindia (04 398 9633, fabindia.com) has one of only two branches outside India in Dubai. A riot of bright colours and subtle hues, the clothing ranges for men and women combine Indian and western styles. The hand-crafted fabrics, including soft furnishings, table cloths and cushion covers, will add an ethnic touch to your home. Similar in style, Mumbai Se carries a range of funky fashions and home decoration pieces by modern Indian designers at its stores in BurJuman, The Dubai Mall, Dubai Marina Mall and Festival Centre.

Elsewhere, fashion boutique S*uce stocks a range of funky accessories, quirky fashions and gifts at its eclectic boutiques in The Village Mall (04 344 7270) and The Dubai Mall (04 339 9696). Fans of designer labels can head out to Boutique 1 on The Walk in JBR (04 425 7888); a bigger branch is located in Mall of the Emirates (04 395 1200). Those looking for home accessories should consider Marina Exotic Home Interiors. The Mall of the Emirates branch (04 341 0314) carries a great range of homewares with distinct regional flair: think colourful cushions, lanterns and elaborate wood carvings. Burlesque (04 346 1616) on Al Wasl Road is an elaborate store with highly romantic furniture and plenty of floral prints. This is the place to head if you are bored with formulaic approaches to interior design and would

Gold & Diamonds

The Gold & Diamond Park (04 347 7788, goldanddiamondpark. com), is a great place to buy jewellery if you are more interested in buying than enjoying the souk experience. There are branches of many of the outlets that are also found in the Gold Souk but here they are much quieter (Map 5 C2).

like some stylish, but eccentric, pieces to take home. Should you be in the market for something more substantial, Pinky Furniture & Novelties (04 422 1720, pinkyfurnitureuae.com) is particularly good for buying Indian teak furniture. The warehouse shop is located in Al Barsha. For home decoration that's easier to carry with you, look no further than Gallery One: this specialist shop carries contemporary, beautifully framed Arabian prints and photography.

There are several branches across town, including stores in Mall of the Emirates (04 341 4488), Souk Madinat Jumeirah (04 368 6055) and The Walk At Jumeirah Beach Residence (04 423 1987). The boho enclave of The Courtyard (courtyard-uae. com) in Al Qouz has funky furniture and accessories amid its art galleries. Traffic (viatraffic.org) is a gallery, gift shop and studio in Al Barsha that stocks fashion items, interior design pieces and small gifts. The Antique Museum (04 347 9935), in Al Qouz, is full to the brim with everything from souvenirs (not all of them from the UAE), to furniture, pashminas and Omani silver. The prices are less than in tourist hotspots like Souk Madinat Jumeirah and wandering through its passageways and secret rooms is a treat in itself. If you've forgot your iPad charger at home, Sharaf DG (sharafdg.com) is one of the more popular spots to buy electronics. You'll find branches in several of the malls but its largest store is in Times Square Center (800 344 357). For something for the kids – or grownups with a soft spot for sweet treats – head to Candylicious (04 330 8700, candyliciousshop.com). This super-sized sweet shop in The Dubai Mall has enough goodies to keep those with a sweet tooth grinning from ear to ear.

Going Out

Dine, Drink, Dance	220
Entertainment	226
Venue Directory	230
Area Directory	236
Restaurants & Cafes	246
Bars, Pubs & Clubs	300

Dine, Drink, Dance

Celebrity chefs, world-class nightlife and ethnic eateries; Dubai's dining and entertainment options are endless.

Dubai's gastronomic landscape is huge and constantly growing. Cosmopolitan culinary treats, picturesque bars and cosy shisha joints combine to form the region's most exciting nightlife. The city's varied population has produced a demand for exceptional food. Fine-dining aficionados will be impressed with the diversity, quality and abundance of first-rate restaurants, while culinary tourists can dine on authentic Arabic kebabs for lunch and fiery Pakistani curries for dinner.

Thursday and Friday nights are the big ones, with reservations required in the restaurants and international DJs in the clubs. However, during the week you'll find drinks deals across the city and all manner of dining promotions. See Brunch & Other Deals for more information. While Dubai doesn't lend itself to pub crawls by foot or evening strolls around restaurant districts, because venues

The Yellow Star
The little yellow star highlights venues that merit extra praise. It could be the atmosphere, the food, the cocktails, the music or the crowd, but whatever the reason, any review that you see with the star attached is for somewhere considered a bit special.

tend to be located in the same building, such as a hotel or a mall such as Souk Madinat Jumeirah. Or, you'll need to take a short taxi ride between bars.

Keep in mind that Dubai's licensing laws are unique. For a venue to serve alcohol, it must be attached to a hotel or a sporting facility. This means no supermarket six-packs and no wine at your independent bistro. The legal drinking age is 21, and it's best to avoid getting staggeringly drunk as it may land you behind bars. Most importantly, don't even think about getting behind the wheel of a car after drinking – Dubai maintains a strict zero tolerance stance on drink driving. Respect the laws and you'll have nothing to worry about – Dubai certainly knows how to throw a party.

Brunch & Other Deals

With so many venues to choose from, Dubai's restaurants and bars face stiff competition in attracting punters. As a result, there are some excellent deals on food and drink almost every day of the week. All-you-can-eat-and-drink deals abound, and some of the city's best restaurants offer time-specific deals that let diners experience exquisite creations at extreme discounts. Tuesday has become the official ladies' night for several of Dubai's drinking institutions, including Healey's and Blends in Marsa Dubai, and Armani/Privé (04 888 3308) in Downtown. Check askexplorer.com for an insider scoop on the latest 'it' venues and the hottest offers when you're in town.

The king of all Dubai deals is the Friday brunch, and a lazy, drawn out, all-you-can-eat-and-drink afternoon is a must for any visitor. Many of the finest five-star hotels, including Al Qasr, Burj Al Arab, Park Hyatt Dubai and Jumeirah Beach Hotel put on lavish spreads every Friday afternoon and they're almost always packed with punters. These all-you-can-eat-and-drink affairs often include unlimited champagne and food from all over the world – sometimes with the option to extend your feast through the evening for an additional fee. Of course, such luxury comes at a price – usually upwards of Dhs.350 for the premium options. If you want to indulge in daytime dining but want to save the dirhams then there are some decent cheaper options, such as Organic Foods & Cafe's Dhs.95 for adults and Dhs.65 for kids option (04 434 0577) and Pergolas (04 321 1111) in the Murooj Rotana, which offers all-you-can-eat-and-drink themed dinner buffets every night of the week.

Double Trouble

Dubai has a number of restaurants that deserve extra credit for their stellar bars. Trader Vic's serves some stunning, strong cocktails, while El Malecon is worth a trip for the bar alone. Likewise, several of Dubai's bars, including Caramel and Sho Cho's serve light bites and bigger plates that are tasty enough to warrant a table reservation.

Vegetarian

There are plenty of delicious local delicacies that will thrill herbivores. *Rahib* salad, a hot combination of aubergine and tomato, is a great option when eating Lebanese food, or you could go with tasty tabouleh, *fattoush* and falafel, all served with fluffy fresh bread. Middle Eastern food traditions aside, the huge population of south Asians means there are plenty of authentic vegetable curries to be had. Head to Karama or Satwa to try a veg thali, which consists of up to 10 small pots of curries, pickles and sauces into which you can dip chapatti, or mix with rice. You'll find plenty of small restaurants in and around Karama; Saravana Bhavan is an exceptionally good choice, and the experience will rarely cost you more than Dhs.12.

Karaoke

The draw of the microphone and the lure of crooning embarrassment is alive and well in Dubai, and the city's best karaoke bars are tight and intimate, just as they should be. Harry Ghatto's (04 319 8088) in Emirates Towers is a favourite, Hibiki (04 317 2221) in Hyatt Regency has private rooms, and It's Mirchi (04 334 4088) offers a bizarre Indian alternative, complete with plenty of curries and a multilingual songbook.

Nightclubs

Massive sound systems, international DJs, incredibly diverse interiors and just enough musical variety to keep things interesting – Dubai's club scene has long been the best in the region, and it keeps getting better. House and popular R&B dominate Dubai's dancefloors, but some clubs regularly promote theme nights such as Arabic, Indian and cheesy music (for the worst kind of cheese, and least pretentious vibe, go to Rock Bottom in TECOM or Bur Dubai). Door policies differ from venue to venue. Some of the most exclusive spots, such as Cavalli Club and Cirque Le Soir Dubai (056 115 4507), won't let you in unless you're on the guest list, while others like Chi@The Lodge merely require a decent pair of shoes.

Street Food

The shawarma is to Dubai what the hot dog is to New York. The popular snack, consisting of rolled pita bread filled with lamb or chicken carved from a rotating spit, can be found throughout the city, and tiny cafeterias serving the delicacy are around every corner. At about Dhs.5 each, they're the perfect end to a big night out or a tasty pre-club snack. Try to avoid shawarma stands that carve from tiny slabs of meat – a huge shawarma spit is a good sign that the cafeteria has a high turnover. Street-side cafeterias also squeeze and press some of the best and least expensive fresh juices in the city.

Shisha

It's common to see people relaxing in the evening with a shisha pipe. Shisha is a popular method of smoking tobacco with a water-filled pipe. It comes in a variety of flavours, including grape and apple. Some of the best places to try shisha in Dubai are Reem Al Bawadi (and QD's at Boardwalk).

Arabian Experience

Al Fanar and Bastakiah Nights are among the handful of restaurants specialising in local Emirati dishes like al *machboos* or al *harees*. In addition, there's plenty of opportunity to experience Arabic food from other parts of the region, especially Lebanon and Syria. Tabouleh (chopped parsley with bulgar, tomato and herbs), *fattoush* (salad seasoned with sumac and topped with toasted pita), *arayes* (grilled flat bread with spiced meat in the middle) and many kinds of grilled, skewered meat can be found in any Arabic restaurant – all of these are great introductions to regional cuisine and no visit should end without sampling the local delicacies at least once. Head to Reem Al Bawadi for an authentic first try, chill out at Al Khayma over shisha and *shish taouk*, or splash out and book a table at an upscale Arabic eatery such as Levantine. For the full Arabian experience, try heading out on a desert safari where you'll be entertained by a belly dancer, dine on a full array of Arabic delights under the stars and smoke the requisite shisha. You can even get a henna tattoo.

All Aboard

Dinner on the creek is a must. While in town, try the five-star fare of Bateaux Dubai (04 814 5553, bateauxdubai. com). Alternatively, opt for Creek Cruises (04 280 7860, creekcruises. com) for the fun tourist option that comes complete with a belly dancer.

Entertainment

With a popular film festival, massive concerts and a growing theatre scene, Dubai is a regional entertainment hub.

Cinema

Dubai loves going to the movies, and the city's residents flock to the cinemas every weekend. The biggest theatres include a 22 screen Reel Cinema outlet in The Dubai Mall (04 449 1988, reelcinemas.ae) and a 21 screen cinema at Ibn Battuta Mall (Novo Megaplex, novocinemas.com). Another major player, VOX Cinemas (voxcinemas.com), also has theatres across town, including ones offering 3D content and premium screenings for select films. Be prepared for people to talk or use their phones during movies though.

Outdoor screenings have become popular of late and movies in the pool has become the latest craze. Wafi launched its Movies Under The Stars in 2010, while Dubai Polo & Equestrian Club (04 361 8111, poloclubdubai.com) and The Address Montgomerie (themontgomerie.com) both offer movie screenings outside by the pool during the hotter summer months.

Dubai cinemas tend to mostly show mainstream films, but movie buffs in town during December are in for a treat. The Dubai International Film Festival (DIFF) is a cinematic highlight that runs for a week across various locations. You can watch an impressive mix of mainstream, world and local cinema – from short films to full-length features.

Comedy

Comedy nights in Dubai are popular with the expat crowd but events tend to be semi-regular, rather than weekly nights. The Laughter Factory (thelaughterfactory.com) organises monthly performances, with comedians from the UK's Comedy Store coming over to play various venues throughout Dubai, including Zinc and The Aviation Club (jumeirah.com). A lot of comedy is aimed at the expat crowd, so unless you're familiar with the comedian's country, you might not be laughing. Keep an eye on thelaughterfactory.com for details of future shows.

Live Music

Dubai hosts a number of concerts each year, and as the city grows it attracts bigger names. Past acts include Muse, Kanye West, Sting and Robbie Williams. The bigger names usually play at outdoor venues such as the Tennis Stadium, Dubai Autodrome and the amphitheatre at Media City.

In addition to acts at the height of their fame, Dubai also plays host to a string of groups that may be past their prime,

Something Different

Many of the nightclubs in Bur Dubai's three and four-star hotels feature live bands that cater for a certain culture. For African music, head to the Beach Club at the Palm Beach Hotel (04 393 1999) and for a lively Filipino band try Maharlika at the President Hotel (04 334 6565).

but nonetheless provide good entertainment (think Human League, Go West, Echo & The Bunnymen and Deacon Blue).

There has been a recent rise in alternative and slightly lesser-known acts coming over for some sun including Groove Armada, 2ManyDJs and Super Furry Animals. Dubai also hosts several music festivals each year focusing on rock, rhythm and world music; and there's the popular Sandance, (sandance.ae) which hosts rock and dance acts. For more information on events in Dubai and Abu Dhabi, see Explorer's website (askexplorer.com) which has details of events, promotions and upcoming gigs in both cities.

Theatre

The theatre scene in Dubai is growing thanks to residents' thirst for culture, and theatre lovers finally have something to cheer about. Madinat Theatre (madinat theatre.com) hosts a variety of performances, from serious stage plays to comedies and musical performances. Cirque du Soleil has set up its massive big-top at Ibn Battuta each spring for the past few years and is always a big hit. The Palladium (palladium-dmc. com), is located in Media City and has hosted acts from Akon to The Wiggles. A local theatre scene is also beginning to thrive – Dubai Community Theatre and Arts Centre (ductac. org) at Mall of the Emirates provides valuable theatre space for amateur dramatics performances, as well as for smaller-scale shows which have included touring shows from Edinburgh's Fringe festival. On the 42nd floor, Dubai's highest theatre, The Act (theactdubai.com), is a cabaret/nightclub hybrid, complimented by an innovative Peruvian restaurant.

Dubai Community Theatre and Arts Centre

Venue Directory

Restaurants & Cafes

Afternoon Tea

Karat	p.271
Lobby Lounge	p.274
Sahn Eddar	p.288

Arabic/Lebanese

Al Khayma	p.247
Al Mallah	p.248
Al Nafoorah	p.249
Arabesque Cafe	p.251
Bastakiah Nights	p.256
Cafe Arabesque	p.260
Fakhreldine	p.264
Levantine	p.273
Reem Al Bawadi	p.285

Argentinean

Asado	p.252

Asian

Bamboo Lagoon	p.256
Beachcombers	p.257
Eauzone	p.262

Cafe

Arabian Tea House	p.251
Counter Culture	p.261
Maison Bagatelle	p.275
Sultan's Lounge	p.292
The Lime Tree Cafe & Kitchen	p.273

Chinese

Ba	p.256
Hakkasan	p.267
Hong Loong	p.268
Long Yin	p.274
Shang Palace	p.290
The China Club	p.261
Zheng He's	p.298

Cuban

El Malecon   p.262

Emirati

Al Fanar Restaurant & Cafe   p.247

European

Nineteen   p.279

French

AOC   p.250
Imperium   p.270
La Petite Maison   p.273
Reflets Par Pierre Gagnaire   p.286
Traiteur   p.296

German

Hofbräuhaus   p.268

Indian

Armani/Amal   p.252
Asha's   p.253
Ashiana   p.253
iZ   p.270
Khazana   p.272
Nina   p.278
Saravana Bhavan   p.289
Signature By Sanjeev Kapoor   p.286
Zafran   p.298

International

Al Dawaar   p.247
Après   p.250
Aquara   p.251
At.mosphere   p.253
Flavours On Two   p.266
Fountain Restaurant   p.266
La Brasserie
  (formerly Rostang)   p.272
Meridien Village Terrace   p.277
Table 9   p.293

	The Farm	p.264
	The Ivy	p.270
	The Market Place	p.276
	The Observatory	p.280
	Yalumba	p.297
Iranian		
	Pars Iranian Kitchen	p.282
Italian		
	Armani/Deli	p.252
	BiCE Mare	p.257
	Bussola	p.260
	Frankie's	p.264
	Jamie's Italian	p.271
	Luciano's	p.274
	Medzo	p.277
	Ronda Locatelli	p.288
	Segreto	p.290
	Splendido Restaurant	p.291
Italian/Asian		
	Taste of Fame	p.294
Japanese		
	ICHO	p.268
	Nobu	p.279
	Okku	p.280
	Tokyo@thetowers	p.295
	Wagamama	p.297
	Yo! Sushi	p.298
	Zuma	p.299
Korean		
	Mannaland Korean Restaurant	p.276
	Sumibiya	p.292
Latin American		
	Pachanga	p.282
	Toro Toro	p.295

Lebanese

	Automatic	p.254

Mediterranean

	Al Muntaha	p.248
	AZ.U.R	p.254
	Boardwalk	p.258
	Glasshouse Brasserie	p.267
	Nasimi Beach	p.278
	Sur Mer (formerly Giannino)	p.293
	Villa Beach	p.296

Middle Eastern

	Nawwara	p.278

Moroccan

	Tagine	p.293

Pakistani

	Ravi Restaurant	p.284

Persian

	Shabestan	p.290

Polynesian

	Trader Vic's	p.295

Russian

	Troyka	p.296

Seafood

	Al Mahara	p.248
	Aprons & Hammers	p.250
	Beach Bar & Grill	p.257
	Blue Flame	p.258
	Fish Market	p.266
	Ossiano	p.280
	Pierchic	p.284
	Salmontini Le Resto	p.289

Singaporean

	Peppercrab	p.284

Steakhouse

	Center Cut	p.261

	Gaucho	p.267
	JW's Steakhouse	p.271
	Manhattan Grill	p.276
	Ruth's Chris Steak House	p.288
	Seafire Steakhouse & Bar	p.289
	The Butcher Shop & Grill	p.260
	The Exchange Grill	p.263
	The Meat Co.	p.277
	West 14th New York Grill & Bar	p.297
Thai		
	Blue Elephant	p.258
	Pai Thai	p.282
	Smiling BKK	p.291
	The Thai Kitchen	p.294
	Thiptara	p.294
Turkish		
	Kosebasi	p.272

Bars, Pubs & Clubs

Bar

	360°	p.300
	Bahri Bar	p.301
	Bar 44	p.302
	Barasti	p.302
	Barzar	p.302
	Belgian Beer Cafe	p.303
	Bidi Bondi	p.303
	Blends	p.303
	Blue Bar	p.304
	Buddha Bar	p.304
	Calabar	p.306
	Caramel Restaurant & Lounge	p.306

	Eclipse Bar	p.308
	Healey's Bar & Terrace	p.308
	Jetty Lounge	p.310
	Neos	p.311
	Nezesaussi Grill	p.311
	Oeno Wine Bar	p.312
	Sanctuary Pool Bar & Lounge	p.312
	Shades	p.313
	Sho Cho	p.313
	Siddharta Lounge By Buddha Bar	p.313
	Skyview Bar	p.314
	The Agency	p.300
	The Hub	p.310
	The Rooftop Terrace & Sports Lounge	p.312
	The Terrace	p.314
	Trader Vic's Mai-Tai Lounge	p.314
	Uptown Bar	p.316
	Voda Bar	p.316
	Warehouse	p.316
	Wavebreaker	p.317
Nightclub		
	Boudoir	p.304
	Cavalli Club	p.306
	Chi@The Lodge	p.307
	Embassy Dubai	p.308
	N'Dulge Nightclub	p.311
	XL Beach Club	p.317
	Zinc	p.317
Pub		
	Dhow & Anchor	p.307
	Double Decker	p.307
	The Irish Village	p.310
	The Underground Pub	p.315

Area Directory

Al Barsha 1
Restaurants

Après	Mall of the Emirates	p.250
Salmontini Le Resto	Mall of the Emirates	p.289
The Butcher Shop & Grill	Mall of the Emirates	p.260

Bars, Pubs & Clubs

Sanctuary Pool Bar & Lounge	Sheraton Dubai Mall of the Emirates	p.312

Al Corniche
Restaurants

Al Dawaar	Hyatt Regency Dubai	p.247

Al Garhoud
Restaurants

Blue Elephant	Al Bustan Rotana	p.258
Blue Flame	Jumeirah Creekside Hotel	p.258
Long Yin	Le Meridien Dubai	p.274
Meridien Village Terrace	Le Meridien Dubai	p.277
Yalumba	Le Meridien Dubai	p.297

Bars, Pubs & Clubs

The Irish Village	Nr Dubai Tennis Stadium	p.310
Warehouse	Le Meridien Dubai	p.316

Al Hudaiba
Restaurants

Al Mallah	2nd December St	p.248

Al Jafiliya
Restaurants

Pars Iranian Kitchen	Nr Chelsea Plaza Hotel	p.282

Al Karama
Restaurants
Saravana Bhavan	Nr Karama Park	p.289

Al Kheeran
Restaurants
Al Fanar Restaurant & Cafe	Dubai Festival City Mall	p.247
Jamie's Italian	Dubai Festival City Mall	p.271
Reflets Par Pierre Gagnaire	InterContinental Festival City Al Badia	p.286

Bars, Pubs & Clubs
Belgian Beer Cafe	Crowne Plaza Dubai Festival City	p.303
Eclipse Bar	InterContinental Dubai Festival City	p.308

Al Muraqqabat
Restaurants
Bamboo Lagoon	JW Marriott Hotel Dubai	p.256
Hofbräuhaus	JW Marriott Hotel Dubai	p.268
JW's Steakhouse	JW Marriott Hotel Dubai	p.271
The Market Place	JW Marriott Hotel Dubai	p.276

Al Raffa
Restaurants
Automatic	Al Khaleej Centre	p.254
Signature By Sanjeev Kapoor	Melia Al Raffa	p.286
Troyka	Ascot Hotel	p.296

Al Rigga
Restaurants

Ashiana	Sheraton Dubai Creek Hotel & Towers	p.253
Fish Market	Radisson Blu Hotel	p.266
Glasshouse Brasserie	Hilton Dubai Creek	p.267
Shabestan	Radisson Blu Hotel	p.290
Sumibiya	Radisson Blu Hotel	p.292
Table 9	Hilton Dubai Creek	p.293
The China Club	Radisson Blu Hotel	p.261

Al Safa 1
Restaurants

| Smiling BKK | Al Wasl Rd Al Wasl | p.291 |

Al Satwa
Restaurants

| Ravi Restaurant | 2nd December St | p.284 |

Al Souk Al Kabeer
Restaurants

| Arabian Tea House | Al Fahidi St | p.251 |
| Bastakiah Nights | Al Fahidi Historical Neighbourhood | p.256 |

Al Sufouh 1
Restaurants

Eauzone	Arabian Court At One&Only Royal Mirage	p.262
Nina	Arabian Court At One&Only Royal Mirage	p.278
Pai Thai	Al Qasr	p.282
Pierchic	Al Qasr	p.284
Segreto	Souk Madinat Jumeirah	p.290

Tagine	The Palace At	
	One&Only Royal Mirage	p.293
Trader Vic's	Souk Madinat Jumeirah	p.295
Zheng He's	Mina A'Salam	p.298

Bars, Pubs & Clubs
Barasti	Le Meridien Mina Seyahi	
	Beach Resort & Marina	p.302
Jetty Lounge	One&Only Royal Mirage	p.310
Oeno Wine Bar	The Westin Dubai Mina Seyahi	
	Beach Resort & Marina	p.312
The Agency	Souk Madinat Jumeirah	p.300
The Rooftop Terrace		
& Sports Lounge	One&Only Royal Mirage	p.312

Al Sufouh 2
Restaurants
Arabesque Cafe	Arjaan By Rotana	
	Dubai Media City	p.251
Beach Bar & Grill	The Palace At	
	One&Only Royal Mirage	p.257

Bars, Pubs & Clubs
| Bahri Bar | Mina A'Salam | p.301 |
| Barzar | Souk Madinat Jumeirah | p.302 |

Al Thanyah 3
Restaurants
| Nineteen | The Address | |
| | Montgomerie Dubai | p.279 |

Al Thanyah 5
Bars, Pubs & Clubs
| Healey's Bar & Terrace | Bonnington Jumeirah | |
| | Lakes Towers | p.308 |

Bur Dubai
Restaurants

Fakhreldine	Movenpick Hotel & Apartments Oud Metha	p.264
Fountain Restaurant	Movenpick Hotel & Apartments Oud Metha	p.266

Burj Khalifa
Restaurants

Armani/Amal	Armani Hotel Dubai	p.252
Armani/Deli	Armani Hotel Dubai	p.252
Asado	The Palace Downtown Dubai	p.252
At.mosphere	Burj Khalifa	p.253
BiCE Mare	Souk Al Bahar	p.257
Karat	The Address Dubai Mall	p.271
Maison Bagatelle	Shk Mohd Bin Rashid Boulevard	p.275
The Meat Co.	Souk Al Bahar	p.277
Thiptara	The Palace Downtown	p.294

Bars, Pubs & Clubs

Calabar	The Address Downtown Dubai	p.306
Neos	The Address Downtown Dubai	p.311
Nezesaussi Grill	Al Manzil Hotel	p.311

Business Bay
Restaurants

Nawwara	JW Marriott Marquis Hotel	p.278

Jumeira 1
Restaurants

Al Khayma	Dubai Marine Beach Resort & Spa	p.247
El Malecon	Dubai Marine Beach Resort & Spa	p.262
Mannaland Korean Restaurant	Al Mina Rd Madinat Dubai Al Melaheyah	p.276
The Lime Tree Cafe & Kitchen	Nr Jumeirah Mosque	p.273

Bars, Pubs & Clubs

Boudoir	Dubai Marine Beach Resort & Spa	p.304
Sho Cho	Dubai Marine Beach Resort & Spa	p.313

Jumeira 3
Restaurants

Reem Al Bawadi	Nr HSBC	p.285
Taste of Fame	Sunset Mall	p.294

Marsa Dubai
Restaurants

AOC	Sofitel Dubai	p.250
Aprons & Hammers	DIMC Marsa Dubai	p.250
Aquara	Dubai Marina Yacht Club	p.251
AZ.U.R	Dubai Marriott Harbour Hotel & Suites	p.254
Bussola	Westin Dubai Mina Seyahi Beach Resort	p.260
Counter Culture	Dubai Marriott Harbour Hotel & Suites	p.261
Frankie's	JBR	p.264

Kosebasi	The Walk at Jumeirah Beach Residence	p.272
Lobby Lounge	The Ritz-Carlton Dubai	p.274
Luciano's	Habtoor Grand Beach Resort & Spa	p.274
Pachanga	Hilton Dubai Jumeirah Resort	p.282
Ruth's Chris Steak House	The Address Dubai Marina	p.288
Splendido Restaurant	The Ritz-Carlton Dubai	p.291
Sur Mer (formerly Giannino)	Meydan Beach	p.293
The Observatory	Dubai Marriott Harbour Hotel & Suites	p.280
Toro Toro	Grosvenor House	p.295
Wagamama	Al Fattan Marine Tower	p.297
Yo! Sushi	Dubai Marina Mall	p.298
Zafran	Dubai Marina Mall	p.298

Bars, Pubs & Clubs

Bar 44	Grosvenor House	p.302
Blends	The Address Dubai Marina	p.303
Buddha Bar	Grosvenor House	p.304
Embassy Dubai	Grosvenor House	p.308
Shades	The Address Dubai Marina	p.313
Siddharta Lounge By Buddha Bar	Grosvenor House	p.313
The Hub	Sofitel Dubai Jumeirah Beach	p.310
The Underground Pub	Habtoor Grand Beach Resort & Spa	p.315
Trader Vic's Mai-Tai Lounge	Al Fattan Marine Tower	p.314
Wavebreaker	Hilton Dubai Jumeirah Resort	p.317
XL Beach Club	Habtoor Grand Beach Resort & Spa	p.317

Nakhlat Jumeira

Restaurants

Ba	Fairmont The Palm Nakhlat Jumeira	p.256
Hong Loong	Palm Jumeirah	p.268
Imperium	Jumeirah Zabeel Saray	p.270
La Brasserie	Atlantis The Palm	p.272
Levantine	Atlantis The Palm	p.273
Nasimi Beach	Atlantis The Palm	p.278
Nobu	Atlantis The Palm	p.279
Ossiano	Atlantis The Palm	p.280
Ronda Locatelli	Atlantis The Palm	p.288
Seafire Steakhouse & Bar	Atlantis The Palm	p.289
Sultan's Lounge	Jumeirah Zabeel Saray	p.292
West 14th New York Grill & Bar	Oceana Residences	p.297

Bars, Pubs & Clubs

Bidi Bondi	Clubhouse Al Manhal	p.303
N'Dulge Nightclub	Atlantis The Palm	p.311
Voda Bar	Jumeirah Zabeel Saray	p.316

Oud Metha

Restaurants

Khazana	Al Nasr Leisureland	p.272

Bars, Pubs & Clubs

Chi@The Lodge	Al Nasr Leisureland	p.307

Port Saeed

Restaurants

Boardwalk	Dubai Creek Golf & Yacht Club	p.258
Cafe Arabesque	Park Hyatt Dubai	p.260
The Thai Kitchen	Park Hyatt Dubai	p.294
Traiteur	Park Hyatt Dubai	p.296

Bars, Pubs & Clubs
| The Terrace | Park Hyatt Dubai | p.314 |

Trade Center 1
Restaurants
Flavours On Two	Towers Rotana	p.266
ICHO	Radisson Royal Hotel	p.268
Okku	The H Hotel Dubai	p.280
Shang Palace	Shangri-La Hotel	p.290
The Exchange Grill	Fairmont Dubai	p.263

Bars, Pubs & Clubs
| Cavalli Club | Fairmont Dubai | p.306 |
| Zinc | Crowne Plaza Dubai | p.317 |

Trade Center 2
Restaurants
Al Nafoorah	Towers	p.249
Center Cut	The Ritz-Carlton	p.261
Hakkasan	Jumeirah Emirates Towers	p.267
The Ivy	Boulevard At Jumeirah Emirates Towers	p.270
Tokyo@thetowers	Boulevard At Jumeirah Emirates Towers	p.295
Zuma	Dubai International Financial Centre (DIFC)	p.299

Bars, Pubs & Clubs
| Blue Bar | Novotel World Trade Centre | p.304 |
| Double Decker | Al Murooj Rotana | p.307 |

Umm Hurair 1
Restaurants
| Peppercrab | Grand Hyatt Dubai | p.284 |

Umm Hurair 2
Restaurants
Asha's	Wafi	p.253
iZ	Grand Hyatt Dubai	p.270
Manhattan Grill	Grand Hyatt Dubai	p.276
Medzo	Umm Hurair 2	p.277

Umm Suqeim 3
Restaurants
Al Mahara	Burj Al Arab	p.248
Al Muntaha	Burj Al Arab	p.248
Beachcombers	Jumeirah Beach Hotel	p.257
Sahn Eddar	Burj Al Arab	p.288
Villa Beach	Jumeirah Beach Hotel	p.296

Bars, Pubs & Clubs
360°	Jumeirah Beach Hotel	p.300
Dhow & Anchor	Jumeirah Beach Hotel	p.307
Skyview Bar	Burj Al Arab	p.314
Uptown Bar	Jumeirah Beach Hotel	p.316

Wadi Al Safa 3
Restaurants
The Farm	Nr Falcon City	p.264

Zaa'beel 2
Restaurants
Gaucho	Dubai International Financial Centre (DIFC)	p.267
La Petite Maison	Dubai International Financial Centre (DIFC)	p.273

Bars, Pubs & Clubs
Caramel Restaurant & Lounge	Dubai International Financial Centre (DIFC)	p.306

Restaurants & Cafes

Dubai's culinary landscape includes everything from mountainous buffet spreads to low-key streetside snacks.

There isn't much you can't find in Dubai when it comes to food; whether it's a quick-fix burger, super fresh fish and chips or sizzling curries, the variety is extraordinary. Dining in one of Dubai's five-star hotel resorts is a must, if only to witness the tremendous variety and quality. Bookings are not always necessary, but it is best to check as hotel guests often get first dibs on the tables and popular restaurants do fill up quickly.

Alternatively, bypass Michelin-starred options and still get fare that is both tasty and easy on the wallet. Visitors should experience some of Dubai's modest, yet vibrant and atmospheric, independent Indian restaurants such as Saravana Bhavan and popular Pakistani restaurant Ravi. There are also several Arabic restaurants that are worth a try. Al Mallah on 2nd December Street in Satwa is a popular spot for pavement dining, shawarmas and juices at very reasonable prices.

When it comes to breakfast and lunch, you can grab a bite at the delightful cafes loved by Dubai's expats such as MORE Cafe (04 343 3779, morecafe.co), Shakespeare & Co. (04 331 1757), Lime Tree Cafe and Epicure (04 323 8888). For real cafe culture Dubai-style, stroll along The Walk at Jumeirah Beach Residence, or The Beach development, which has recently been completed opposite. Both developments has a wide selection of restaurants and cafes, and plenty of opportunity to people-watch along the bustling beachfront promenade.

Al Dawaar
International

Hyatt Regency Dubai, Corniche Deira
04 317 2222

Revolving restaurant may evoke images or pure kitsch, but Al Dawaar is a surprisingly sophisticated buffet haunt and the slow revolution (it takes one hour and 45 minutes to do a complete turn) gives you an interesting window on this side of town.

Map 4 D1 **Metro** Palm Deira

Al Fanar Restaurant & Cafe
Emirati

Dubai Festival City Mall, Al Kheeran
04 232 9966

Ask to be seated in one of the *majlis* (tent) spots here and while away the hours sipping tea and relaxing. The indoor section reveals a bustling scene from the old town where you can take your pick and enjoy lunch or dinner at the Pearl Merchants House, Bait Al Tawash (courtyard) or Souk. Each offers a fabulous setting for your meal, and the food itself is a superb introduction to traditional Emirati food.

Map 1 J4 **Metro** Emirates

Al Khayma
Arabic/Lebanese

Dubai Marine Beach Resort & Spa, Jumeira 1
04 346 1111

Turn up at this popular Lebanese haunt for a small bite of Beirut – the atmosphere is lively, and the tempting sofas perfect for whiling away the hours over shisha, drinks and tasty Levantine bites: the veggie platter with dips is the way to go for starters before tucking into piping-hot barbecue grub and shish kebabs. Wash it all down with fresh juices or opt for Lebanese wine. **Map** 1 H2 **Metro** Al Jafiliya

Al Mahara

Seafood

Burj Al Arab, Umm Suqeim 3   04 301 7600

Your visit to Al Mahara starts with a simulated submarine ride that takes you 'under the sea' to dine among the fish. 'Disembark' and you'll see the restaurant is curled around a huge aquarium. This is fine dining at its finest, with prices to match. Gentlemen are required to wear a jacket for dinner.

Map 3 E1 **Metro** Mall of the Emirates

Al Mallah

Arabic/Lebanese

2nd December St, Al Hudaiba   04 398 4723

Al Mallah offers great pavement dining with an excellent view of the world and his brothers cruising by in their Ferraris. The shawarmas and fruit juices are excellent, the cheese and *zatar manoushi* breads exceedingly tasty, and it has possibly the biggest and best falafel in Dubai. The incongruous 'Diana' and 'Charles' shakes are recommended.

Map 1 H2 **Metro** Al Jafiliya

Al Muntaha

Mediterranean

Burj Al Arab, Umm Suqeim 3   04 301 7600

If you weren't at the top of the Burj Al Arab, with an unrivalled view of Dubai's coastline, you would be forgiven for thinking this restaurant's decor is a bit tacky considering the price tag. The menu is less surprising than the decor, with the usual suspects in a European fine-dining line-up. However, the food is certainly good, despite an atmosphere akin to a private members' club.

Map 3 E1 **Metro** Mall of the Emirates

Al Mahara

Al Nafoorah

Arabic/Lebanese

Boulevard At Jumeirah Emirates
Towers, Trade Center 2

04 319 8088

The menu at this highly rated Lebanese restaurant is extensive, with pages and pages of mezze and mains to tantalise. It's best to come in a group and share the wide selection. After dinner, you can take advantage of one of Dubai's few pedestrian areas and take a stroll round The Boulevard, or sit out and enjoy a shisha in front of the looming Emirates Towers.

Map 2 D2 **Metro** Emirates Towers

AOC
French

Sofitel Dubai, Jumeirah Beach, Marsa Dubai   04 448 4848

The staff are friendly and the venue, especially the terrace, make AOC a good dining option in JBR – as long as you arrive with the awareness that the a la carte menu features largely European main courses rather than anything authentically French. However, the quality of food is excellent and the wine list and desserts do their best to return a touch of Gallic oooh la la to proceedings.

Map 3 A1 **Metro** Jumeirah Lakes Towers

Après
International

Mall of the Emirates, Al Barsha 1   04 341 2575

This cosy alpine ski lodge has a comfortable bar area and an unrivalled view of the Ski Dubai slope. The varied menu offers wholesome fare including steaks, fondue and excellent pizzas. During the day, it's great for families but, at night, the laidback vibe and cocktail list encourage chilled dining and socialising. **Map** 3 E2 **Metro** Mall of the Emirates

Aprons & Hammers
Seafood

DIMC Marsa Dubai   04 454 7097

Soak up some incredible views on board this traditional dhow – from the dazzling skyscrapers of Marsa Dubai, to the Palm Jumeirah stretching out to sea. A visit here is a true must-do for seafood fans – armed with a wooden hammer and a giant bib, diners are served huge buckets of delicious crab and other fresh catch, and invited to get cracking.

Map 1 L4 **Metro** DAMAC

Aquara
International

Dubai Marina Yacht Club, Marsa Dubai
04 362 7900

Chic but understated, Aquara allows the view of million-dirham yachts to speak for itself. The menu features options that range from sophisticated burgers to chic, lighter fare with a definite emphasis on seafood, most of which comes with an Asian twist.

Map 3 A1 **Metro** Jumeirah Lakes Towers

Arabesque Cafe
Arabic/Lebanese

Arjaan By Rotana Dubai Media City,
 Al Sufouh 1
04 436 0000

Decorated in the style of a traditional Arabian palace – and enhanced by ornate lighting, plush, purple soft furnishings, traditional ornaments and decorative touches – this pleasant restaurant specialises in Middle Eastern fare. It's mainly a buffet format, including a breakfast and lunch buffet, as well as the Friday brunch.

Map 3 B1 **Metro** Nakheel

Arabian Tea House
Cafe

Al Fahidi St, Al Souk Al Kabeer
04 353 5071

This courtyard cafe and gallery offers quiet sanctuary amid the busy and atmospheric Al Fahidi Historical Neighbourhood. Feel like you've found a piece of Arabia that time forgot as you sit on *majlis*-style cushions or under a canopy while choosing from the healthy dishes and fresh juices; the Arabic breakfast is a good option if you're in this area in the morning. **Map** 4 C2 **Metro** Al Fahidi

Armani/Amal
Indian

Armani Hotel Dubai, Downtown Dubai,
 Burj Khalifa
04 888 3888

The Armani Hotel's Indian restaurant was always going to be a special place, and it has been a huge success, winning awards and admirers from the day it opened. With its open kitchen and vaulted framework, the dining room evokes a hip nightspot in a converted Indian marketplace. Orange and blue lightshades brighten the Armani colour palette and the food is vibrant high-end Indian cuisine.
Map 2 B2 **Metro** Burj Khalifa/Dubai Mall

Armani/Deli
Italian

Armani Hotel Dubai, Downtown Dubai,
 Burj Khalifa
04 888 3888

In keeping with the Armani style of less-is-more, this black and white restaurant's decor is like the food on offer: simple and tasty, beautifully presented Italian fare. Diners can choose to go a la carte or opt for the sharing concept, a set menu that takes you on a culinary journey through the boot country. In addition to Italian treats, there's also a selection of Arabic meats and sweets. **Map** 2 B2 **Metro** Burj Khalifa/Dubai Mall

Asado
Argentinean

The Palace Downtown Dubai,
 Downtown Dubai, Burj Khalifa
04 888 3444

A combination of moody lighting, passionate music, a killer location and a meat lovers' dream menu cement Asado's position as one of Dubai's top steakhouses. Add to this

the superb wine list and terrace views of Burj Khalifa and you've got a formula that makes this Argentinean restaurant something very special.
Map 2 B3 **Metro** Burj Khalifa/Dubai Mall

Asha's
Indian

Wafi, Umm Hurair 2 · 04 324 4100

Owned by Indian superstar Asha Bhosle, this Dubai favourite offers a memorable dining experience. Decked out in summer colours of reds, yellows, and oranges, the space features beaded curtains, low-level lighting, and intimate booths as well as an inviting terrace. The menu features a few Indian favourites plus a selection of Asha's very own signature dishes picked up on her travels.
Map 4 B5 **Metro** Healthcare City

Ashiana
Indian

Sheraton Dubai Creek Hotel & Towers, Al Rigga · 04 207 1733

With empire-inspired decor and a traditional band playing authentic tunes every night, Ashiana celebrates India's colonial era. Cosy booths around the walls are the seats of choice, unless you're in a large group. The staff deserve a special mention for their swift and friendly service.
Map 4 D3 **Metro** Union

At.mosphere
International

Burj Khalifa, Downtown Dubai, Burj Khalifa · 04 888 3444

The world's highest restaurant was always going to be big on the wow factor, but the kitchen manages to deliver on the

lofty ambition with opulent menus of premium ingredients and exquisite presentation. Open for lunch and dinner, this really is the ultimate in high-end dining destinations – and has to be the finest sundowner spot anywhere. Don't forget to take your camera for photos of Dubai 'from the top' and the impressive dancing fountains way, way below.
Map 2 B2 **Metro** Burj Khalifa/Dubai Mall

Automatic
Lebanese

Al Khaleej Centre, Al Raffa   04 355 0333

This popular chain continues to serve high-quality Arabic food in various locations in Dubai. The vast range of mezze is accompanied by mountainous portions of salad, and grilled meat, fish and kebabs. The atmosphere is minimalist but clean and bright, with family-friendly amenities and good service. **Map** 4 B2 **Metro** Al Fahidi

AZ.U.R
Mediterranean

Dubai Marriott Harbour Hotel
  & Suites, Marsa Dubai   04 319 4794

AZ.U.R offers a range of simple but tasty meat, fish and seafood dishes, as well as fresher-than-fresh vegetables, all served in a non-fussy style that lets the ingredients do the talking. The menu features cuisine of France, Morocco, Spain and Italy – think hearty onion soup, mezze, deep-fried calamari and Bolognaise. The sizeable portions are unlikely to leave you hungry and you can digest it all while enjoying a shisha on the large terrace, which boasts lovely views to boot.
Map 3 B1 **Metro** DAMAC

Bastakiah Nights

Ba

Chinese

Fairmont The Palm Nakhlat Jumeira   04 457 3338

Upstairs is a sumptuous lounge serving cocktails topped in gold leaf, while downstairs the vast oriental restaurant sprawls out onto a wonderfully situated terrace with sea views as far as Marsa Dubai. Chefs from all provinces of China showcase their unique skills in a range of Chinese cuisine. **Map** 1 M3 **Metro** Nakheel

Bamboo Lagoon

Asian

JW Marriott Hotel Dubai, Al Muraqqabat   04 607 7977

With a little bridge and a big crocodile, you won't forget this restaurant's decor in a hurry. The food is memorable too: there's sushi, tempura, teriyaki, curries, steaks, stir-fries, grills, seafood, rice and noodle dishes. All are equally tempting and so wonderfully presented that you'll wish you hadn't eaten that big lunch. At 9pm a band takes to the stage and grass-skirted singers serenade diners with low-key renditions of tropical tunes. **Map** 4 E4 **Metro** Abu Baker Al Siddique

Bastakiah Nights

Arabic/Lebanese

Al Fahidi Historical Neighbourhood,
  Al Souk Al Kabeer   04 353 7772

As you enter through heavy wooden doors you are reminded that, despite the glitzy malls and luxurious hotels, Dubai is still very much Arabia. The regional fare on offer is faultless and you can choose between fixed menus and a la carte offerings such as lamb stew and stuffed vine leaves. There's no licence to serve alcohol. **Map** 4 C2 **Metro** Al Fahidi

Beach Bar & Grill
Seafood

The Palace At One&Only Royal Mirage,
Al Sufouh 1
04 399 9999

This superb restaurant is great for a romantic evening. Terrace
tables are candle-lit, and the fresh fish is cooked simply
but with style. Seafood platters to share, and surf and turf
options, are available for people who simply can't pick just
one dish. **Map** 3 B1 **Metro** Nakheel

Beachcombers
Asian

Jumeirah Beach Hotel, Umm Suqeim 3
04 406 8999

This breezy shack has an idyllic location right on the beach
with fantastic views of the Burj Al Arab. Expect excellent Far
Eastern buffets with live cooking stations for stir-fries and
noodles. The Peking duck, curry hotpots and satay are highly
recommended.

Map 3 A1 **Metro** Mall of the Emirates

BiCE Mare
Italian

Souk Al Bahar, Downtown Dubai, Burj Khalifa
04 423 0982

An idyllic location, delicious dishes in all shapes, sizes, both
simple and complex, and an intimate yet relaxed atmosphere
all combine to make this Mediterranean restaurant a serious
contender in Souk Al Bahar. Dine inside and be entertained
by the sultry jazz hands of the resident pianist or take in the
splendid Dubai Fountain show from the terrace. A sister to
BiCE, the Mare signifies a seafood dominated menu that will
bring fish lovers back time and time again.

Map 2 B3 **Metro** Burj Khalifa/Dubai Mall

Blue Elephant

Thai

Al Bustan Rotana, Al Garhoud   04 282 0000

If a trip to Thailand is out of the question, walking into Blue Elephant comes a close second. While sitting at bamboo tables, gazing into a lagoon and surrounded by tropical greenery, the smell of orchids is evocative of exotic Far Eastern climes and the menu showcases an array of Thai classics, which can be spiced to your liking.

Map 4 E6 **Metro** GGICO

Blue Flame

Seafood

Jumeirah Creekside Hotel, Al Garhoud   04 230 8580

The flagship restaurant of Jumeirah Creekside specialises in creative seafood and steak dishes. Head here for a fine-dining experience with refreshingly innovative culinary touches, evident in combinations such as savoury muffins with shiitake mushrooms and broccoli, served with lobster butter.

Map 4 D6 **Metro** GGICO

Boardwalk

Mediterranean

Dubai Creek Golf & Yacht Club, Port Saeed   04 295 6000

Positioned on wooden stilts over the creek, Boardwalk boasts a view that is virtually unmatched in Dubai – and the menu can't be faulted either. Varied enough to suit all tastes, it features a range of international dishes and the drinks list is equally extensive: there's a huge selection of cocktails and mocktails. Just next door sits QD's, which shares the same incredible views but concentrates more on drinks and shisha.

Map 4 C6 **Metro** Deira City Centre

Clockwise from top left: Blue Elephant, Bussola, Boardwalk

Bussola
Italian

Westin Dubai Mina Seyahi Beach Resort
& Marina, Al Sufouh 1 04 511 7136

Famed for its pizzas, Bussola is a longstanding favourite
among the locals. A Sicilian influence on the menu means
the choices are slightly more adventurous than your standard
Italian fare. The open-air first-floor veranda serves cocktails to
a backdrop of sparkling sea views and chill-out tunes.
Map 3 B1 **Metro** Nakheel

The Butcher Shop & Grill
Steakhouse

Mall of the Emirates, Al Barsha 1 04 347 1167

Shoppers with a taste for hearty meat dishes need not look
further than this Kempinski joint with easy access from Mall
of the Emirates: pick your fillet, rump, T-bone or prime rib and
watch in awe as the giant man-size portions are served up.
This is also a good option should you get hungry during an
afternoon spent in the cool climes of Ski Dubai.
Map 3 E2 **Metro** Mall of the Emirates

Cafe Arabesque
Arabic/Lebanese

Park Hyatt Dubai, Port Saeed 04 317 2222

Here you can choose from a buffet or an a la carte menu,
with typical Arabic dishes including a cold mezze spread,
succulent wood-fired kebabs and other, fantastic Lebanese,
Syrian and Jordanian dishes. To top off the experience, there
are marvellous views of the creek, and the restaurant has
perfect romantic, soft ambient lighting.
Map 4 C5 **Metro** GGICO

Center Cut
Steakhouse

The Ritz-Carlton, Dubai International
Financial Centre, Trade Center 2   04 372 2323

Located close to DIFC, this is a good option for carnivores
in the heart of Dubai's financial district. The restaurant's
speciality is evident from the start: the first page of the menu
is adorned with a diagram of a cow and the cuts of meat,
and while the appetisers include non-carnivorous items such
as Atlantic salmon and foie gras, your main meal is really all
about the steaks here. Choose from Australian or American
cuts with a selection of sauces and sides to accompany your
chosen one. **Map** 2 D2 **Metro** Financial Centre

The China Club
Chinese

Radisson Blu Hotel, Dubai Deira Creek, Al Rigga   04 205 7033

A chic space, with subtle touches of authenticity, serving
familiar favourites from all over China. The Peking duck,
carved at the table, is a great choice from the a la carte menu,
while the daily lunchtime buffet, Yum Cha, offers excellent
value: for Dhs.99, you get to sample a feast of dim sum,
noodles and other Chinese specialities, along with tea and
soft drinks. **Map** 4 D2 **Metro** Union

Counter Culture
Cafe

Dubai Marriott Harbour Hotel & Suites,
Marsa Dubai   04 319 4793

Deli delights and easy-going vibes lie within this little gem of
a cafe in Dubai Marina. The cosy joint features relaxing leather
chairs, wooden furniture and a contemporary colour scheme.

The bread is guaranteed to be freshly-baked – so much so that you can actually watch it being prepared. In addition, daily hot and cold specials, big salads, chunky sandwiches and home-made icecream is what's on offer here. The venue is licensed and open from 6am to 5pm.
Map 3 B1 **Metro** DAMAC

Eauzone
Asian
Arabian Court At One&Only Royal Mirage,
Al Sufouh 1
04 399 9999
One of the most romantic restaurants in Dubai, Eauzone has poolside tables, low lighting and sublime flavours, all enhanced by soft background music. The setting is absolutely stunning and the dresscode is smart/casual. The Asian inspired options include sushi, scallops, risotto and Thai prawns but, with curve balls such as foie gras thrown in, you'll find seducing surprises too.
Map 3 C1 **Metro** Nakheel

El Malecon
Cuban
Dubai Marine Beach Resort & Spa, Jumeira 1   04 346 1111
El Malecon's high turquoise walls, big windows that overlook a glowing lagoon and low lighting create a sultry Cuban atmosphere that builds up slowly during the course of the evening, helped along by the live music and Salsa dancers. The menu isn't the longest you'll see (the signature paella is the best choice), but the lively vibe makes up for it – you'll feel completely in the holiday mood.
Map 1 H2 **Metro** World Trade Centre

Fakhreldine

The Exchange Grill

Steakhouse

Fairmont Dubai, Trade Center 1   04 311 8316

The Exchange Grill is the epitome of excess with outsized leather armchairs, modern art installations and a floor-to-ceiling chandelier. The menu strikes a balance between classicism and innovation, and both the lunch and dinner menus offer the best-quality beef.

Map 2 E1 **Metro** World Trade Centre

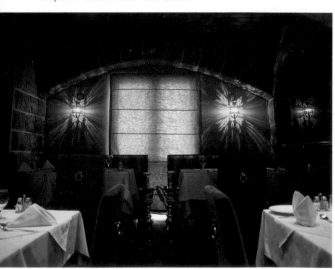

Fakhreldine
Arabic/Lebanese

Movenpick Hotel & Apartments
Oud Metha, Bur Dubai
04 336 6000

From your first dip into the creamy hummus to the last crumb of Arabic sweets, the quality is apparent and the bill isn't too painful to stomach either. Choose from rarer Arabic dishes and old favourites as you watch the gyrating belly dancer strut her stuff to exotic tunes. **Map** 4 B5 **Metro** Oud Metha

The Farm
International

Nr Falcon City, Wadi Al Safa 3
04 392 5660

Located within the fancy residential district of Al Barari, this new restaurant lies a good 20-30 minute drive outside the city. However, the trek is worth it if you'd like to sample locally produced food in a stylish setting that's tranquil enough to make it feel like a real escape from the bright lights of Dubai. With plenty of healthy meals on the menu, this is also a good option for anyone watching their waistline.
Map 1 F5

Frankie's
Italian

JBR, Marsa Dubai
04 399 4311

Grab a vodka Martini and pizza in the bar at this stylish joint, co-owned by Frankie Dettori and Marco Pierre White, then head into the main restaurant for classic Italian dishes and new favourites such as duck ravioli. With its sultry interior, pianist and good quality Friday brunch, this is a classy establishment with a welcoming vibe.
Map 1 K5 **Metro** Jumeirah Lakes Towers

Fish Market

Fish Market
Seafood
Radisson Blu Hotel, Dubai Deira Creek, Al Rigga   04 222 7171

This is the destination of choice for seafood aficionados. Accompanied by a member of staff clad in plastic gloves and clutching a wicker shopping basket, you can select fresh fish, then request the style of cooking. While you wait for your tailor-made dinner to arrive, you can snack on a bowl of french fries and soak up the creekside view.

Map 4 D2 **Metro** Union

Flavours On Two
International
Towers Rotana, Trade Center 1   04 312 2202

This stylish, busy 'dinner brunch' venue focuses on a different global cuisine each night, including British and Italian. The wide range of dishes includes cold starters, hot grills and delicious desserts. Free-flowing alcohol is included in the reasonable cover charge, or you can upgrade to champagne by forking out a few extra dirhams.

Map 2 C1 **Metro** Financial Centre

Fountain Restaurant
International
Movenpick Hotel & Apartments
 Oud Metha, Bur Dubai   04 310 4320

The Movenpick Bur Dubai may be an established hotel, but their new Full Monty Brunch is a welcome addition: the weekend brunch is a truly British feast, with typical pub grub expertly delivered – indeed, it is the sheer size of their signature fry-up that draws in the crowd.

Map 4 B5 **Metro** Oud Metha

Gaucho

Steakhouse

Dubai International Financial Centre,
  Zaa'beel 2

04 422 7898

This Argentinian-inspired steakhouse caters for carnivores
with a soft-spot for trendy settings and Latin culinary
touches. The ultra-modern decor comes complete with
rustic cowhide upholstery, while items such as chimichurri
add an exotic twist to the menu. Gaucho is set on two floors
with differing vibes; the restaurant itself is downstairs, while
the upstairs lounge offers a bar menu and drinks.

Map 2 D2 **Metro** Emirates Towers

Glasshouse Brasserie

Mediterranean

Hilton Dubai Creek, Al Rigga

04 227 1111

Sample a taste of the Mediterranean at this chic brasserie
with glass walls, dark woods, tasteful colours and Mondrian-
style paintings. The menus provides contemporary dishes
with a touch of flair. It's a good spot for a business lunch or a
lively group dinner. The brunch is also worthwhile.

Map 4 D3 **Metro** Al Rigga

Hakkasan

Chinese

Jumeirah Emirates Towers, Trade Center 2

04 384 8484

Hakkasan's sleek decor fuses familiar Hakkasan design
with Dubai-esque touches in this high-end venue with a
spectacular terrace. The menu is faithful to the tried-and-
tested Hakkasan formula: opt for dim sum, crispy duck salad
or the stewed wagyu beef, you're unlikely to be disappointed.

Map 2 D2 **Metro** Emirates Towers

Hofbräuhaus
German

JW Marriott Hotel Dubai, Al Muraqqabat
04 607 7977

From the sauerkraut to the white sausage with sweet mustard, everything here is authentically Bavarian. Add in the beer hall decor, traditional garb for the staff and accordion music and you have a recipe for a fun night out. Several German beers are on tap, along with a full selection of wines.
Map 4 E4 **Metro** Abu Baker Al Siddique

Hong Loong
Chinese

Sofitel The Palm Resort & Spa,
Palm Jumeirah, Nakhlat Jumeira
04 455 6677

A delectable dining experience in a beautiful setting that transports you immediately to a sophisticated China. There's a varied menu with specialities including traditional clay pot dishes as well as inspirational desserts served on plates of steaming dry ice. Staff are knowledgeable about the history, culture and customs behind each dish. There's even a resident Tea Sommelier. **Map** 1 D1 **Metro** Nakheel

ICHO
Japanese

Radisson Royal Hotel, Trade Center 1
04 308 0550

This is an upmarket but relaxed restaurant where even Japanese food aficionados can discover new flavours and textures in dishes that are nothing short of a work of art. Each plate is balanced and intricate, yet contains just the right portion sizes to enable you to enjoy five courses. Service is excellent and there are superb views of Dubai's twinkling lights. **Map** 2 E1 **Metro** World Trade Centre

Hong Loong

Imperium
French

Jumeirah Zabeel Saray,
 Palm Jumeirah, Nakhlat Jumeira   04 453 0444

This French restaurant with gigantic pillars and crystal chandeliers is headed by Jean Hurstel, a talented chef whose skills in Parisian cuisine transcend into the main courses, all of which are served in a petite stainless steel pan, making it easy to pass around for guests to share. However, they are so good, you may not want to share! **Map** 1 C2 **Metro** Nakheel

The Ivy
International

Boulevard At Jumeirah Emirates Towers,   04 319 8767
 Trade Center 2

The Ivy's modern, brasserie-style menu is loyal to the original London venue: British treats from fish and chips to porkbelly and black pudding are executed with finesse, as are the lighter options that feature many Thai-inspired fusion creations. With tinted glass and green leather, the decor is equally evocative of the original West End setting.
Map 2 D2 **Metro** Emirates Towers

iZ
Indian

Grand Hyatt Dubai, Umm Hurair 2   04 317 2222

iZ's dark, contemporary interior is a beautifully designed space, complete with hardwood screens, sculptures and private rooms. The traditional tandoor dishes are presented tapas style – ideal for sampling several flavours. Expect gourmet Indian cuisine with authenticity.
Map 4 B6 **Metro** Healthcare City

Jamie's Italian

Italian

Dubai Festival City Mall, Al Kheeran   04 232 9969

British celebrity chef, crusader for organic food and saviour of school dinners, Jamie Oliver has decided to go for the mid-range family market at his namesake Dubai haunt. The menu features antipasti and a selection of tasty pastas, while the mains cover the usual suspects – a burger, steak and Jamie's signature baked fish parcel. There's also a venue in Jumeirah Beach Hotel. **Map** 1 J4 **Metro** Emirates

JW's Steakhouse

Steakhouse

JW Marriott Hotel Dubai, Al Muraqqabat   04 607 7977

Set in an intimate, secluded part of the hotel, at JW's Steakhouse you are greeted by the sight of chefs slicing huge chunks of meat in the open kitchen. Once you are shown to your stately leather armchair, a huge menu offering an impressive range of steak and seafood awaits.
Map 4 E4 **Metro** Abu Baker Al Siddique

Karat

Afternoon Tea

The Address Dubai Mall,
  Downtown Dubai, Burj Khalifa   04 438 8888

Afternoon tea doesn't come much more professional than this. You get to choose from a vast selection of 26 teas, and the sides are served in four courses starting with scones, madeleines, jams and Devonshire cream; then a selection of bite size finger sandwiches arrive, followed by an array of miniature cakes, pastries and Arabic sweets.
Map 2 C2 **Metro** Burj Khalifa/Dubai Mall

Khazana
Indian

Al Nasr Leisureland, Oud Metha · 04 336 0061

Indian celebrity chef Sanjeev Kapoor's spacious, popular eatery specialises in cuisine from northern India. All dishes are well-prepared and served in big portions, but the prawn curry and chicken tikka are the most popular. Other delicacies include grilled tandoori seafood, a variety of rice dishes and some hearty gravy options. **Map** 4 B4 **Metro** Oud Metha

Kosebasi
Turkish

The Walk at Jumeirah Beach Residence · 04 439 3788

Kosebasi's friendly staff take you on a culinary tour of Anatolia right in the heart of JBR Walk. The mezze, breads and kebabs all have a hint of familiarity, but are surprisingly different to standard Arabic fare, offering a welcome choice. Outside, the pavement terrace is bustling and the beach is just across the road.

Map 3 A1 **Metro** DAMAC

La Brasserie (formerly Rostang)
International

Atlantis The Palm, Nakhlat Jumeira · 04 426 2626

La Brasserie's modern and friendly atmosphere make you feel at home as soon as you walk through the door. Chef de Cuisine Aaron Gillespie has created a menu featuring the highest quality prime and secondary cuts, along with innovative dishes including Saltbush Lamb, Pumpkin Pearl Barley Risotto, and the decadent D.I.Y Injection. It's a friendly venue to pop into for the daily crepe and coffee offer too.

Map 1 C1 **Metro** Nakheel

La Petite Maison
French

Dubai International Financial Centre (DIFC),
Zaa'beel 2
04 439 0505

This classy, unfussy restaurant is like a clean, white canvas on which the dining experience can paint itself. The French staff, dressed in bow ties and stripy aprons flit between tables as the chefs beaver away in the open kitchen. The menu features typically Gallic dishes without the cliches – this is the real deal – simple and delicious food with uncomplicated flavours, in which the high-quality fresh produce speaks volumes.
Map 2 C2 **Metro** Financial Centre

Levantine
Arabic/Lebanese

Atlantis The Palm, Palm Jumeirah, Nakhlat Jumeira   04 426 2626

This is one of Dubai's ultimate upscale Lebanese dining venues. Popular set menus provide a delicious spread of mezze, mains and desserts, and an extensive a la carte menu allows the more adventurous to try new dishes. The wine list includes some Lebanese delights, while belly dancing and shisha complete the experience. **Map** 1 C1 **Metro** Nakheel

The Lime Tree Cafe & Kitchen
Cafe

Nr Jumeirah Mosque, Jumeira 1
04 349 8498

Set in a converted villa on Jumeira Road, this impressive cafe has become a Dubai institution and a firm favourite among the local expat ladies (also known as 'Jumeira Janes'). The understated interior features trendy plastic chairs, dark wood tables and lime-green washed walls. With a definite nod towards Mediterranean cuisine, there's plenty of paninis filled with wholesome ingredients, as well as delicious couscous salads and satay kebabs – and quite possibly the best carrot cake in the city. The coffee is also worth a special mention. **Map** 1 H2 **Metro** Al Jafiliya

Lobby Lounge

Afternoon Tea

The Ritz-Carlton Dubai, Marsa Dubai

04 399 4000

Tea at the Ritz is an exquisite experience. Delicate finger sandwiches and dainty pastries, succulent scones with clotted cream and a selection of jams, a fabulously colonial selection of teas and the fine china are all deliciously regal. It feels exclusive, but all are welcome. **Map** 3 A1 **Metro** DAMAC

Long Yin

Chinese

Le Meridien Dubai, Al Garhoud

04 217 0000

This perennial Chinese favourite has recently gone through a revamp and, in addition to a sleek new decor, it now boasts one of the best dim sum selections in Dubai. The rest of the menu features skillfully prepared Cantonese and Schezwan favourites and the quality of the food remains top-notch. **Map** 4 E6 **Metro** Airport Terminal 1

Luciano's

Italian

Habtoor Grand Beach Resort & Spa, Marsa Dubai

04 399 5000

Good-quality dishes from across Italy are served at this pleasant poolside restaurant. The portions are generous; the starters, ranging from *calamari fritti* to mozzarella and tomato, are particularly noteworthy in this regard. The real star of the

The Lobby Lounge

show, however, is the selection of thin-crust pizzas, which are among the best in town. When the weather is conducive, ask for a table outside underneath the fairy-light bedecked palm trees. **Map** 3 B1 **Metro** DAMAC

Maison Bagatelle

Cafe

Shk Mohd Bin Rashid Boulevard,
 Downtown Dubai, Burj Khalifa   04 420 3442

A fresh, vibrant and sophisticated cafe with reasonable prices and a Parisian vibe, serving an array of breakfasts, salads, crepes and evening meals of an exceptional standard. Be sure to try the French pastries and specialist coffee menu. Floor-to-ceiling windows look out to the terrace and the queue of people eager to gain entry. **Map** 4 E6 **Metro** GGICO

Mannaland Korean Restaurant
Korean
Al Mina Rd, Madinat Dubai Al Melaheyah   04 345 1300

A real find, for a truly unique Dubai dining experience, this Korean restaurant in Satwa offers traditional floor seating and excellent, authentic food cooked right there at your table. This is the place to try *kimchi* – a dish made of fermented vegetables, said to be a superfood. Wash it all down with a teapot of 'special brew'. Great value too.

Map 2 J4   **Metro** Al Jafiliya

Manhattan Grill
Steakhouse
Grand Hyatt Dubai, Umm Hurair 2   04 317 2222

Compared to the indoor rainforest of the hotel's lobby, Manhattan Grill is the ultimate in low-key chic. Soft lighting, plush seating, smooth music and an excellent selection of succulent steaks make this a good choice for fine dining in a very pleasant setting.

Map 4 B6   **Metro** Healthcare City

The Market Place
International
JW Marriott Hotel Dubai, Al Muraqqabat   04 607 7977

Friendly and welcoming, The Market Place is another of Dubai's top all-you-can-eat restaurants. Go with a very empty belly as no sooner have you sat down than the waiter brings what will undoubtedly be the first beverage of many. However, it's the food that distinguishes this buffet restaurant which has live cooking stations and a most impressive buffet of starters and desserts.

Map 4 E4   **Metro** Abu Baker Al Siddique

The Meat Co.

Steakhouse

Souk Al Bahar, Downtown Dubai, Burj Khalifa   04 420 0737

This popular South African chain is more than just a string of
steakhouses. Start with a mezze appetiser platter, then move
on to a lamb skewer with peppers, or an enormous steak
with your choice of carbs. There is another restaurant at Souk
Madinat Jumeirah (04 368 6040); the alfresco setting by the
canals makes it a great choice which you can follow up with a
stroll around the souk's waterside pathways.

Map 2 B3 **Metro** Burj Khalifa/Dubai Mall

Medzo

Italian

Umm Hurair 2   04 324 4100

Back with a new look and a new, longer menu, Medzo still
delivers the same splendid gastronomy. Elegant white
mixes with chandeliers and dreamy drapes to create a more
romantic atmosphere set to a soundtrack of soft piano. When
the weather permits, the tree-shaded terrace completes the
experience. **Map** 4 B5 **Metro** Dubai Healthcare City

Meridien Village Terrace

International

Le Meridien Dubai, Al Garhoud   04 702 2455

Only open in winter and beautifully lit at night, this large
space manages to feel intimate for couples but is also perfect
for larger groups. Each night there is a different culinary
theme: Caribbean, Mexican, BBQ or Arabic. Numerous live-
cooking stations keep the food wonderfully fresh, while the
drinks are replenished with alarming regularity.

Map 4 E6 **Metro** Airport Terminal 1

Nasimi Beach

Mediterranean

Atlantis, The Palm, Palm Jumeirah, Nakhlat Jumeira 04 426 2626

Nasimi's formula is simple: it fuses party vibes with a small menu of seafood and meat coupled with one of the best alfresco settings in the city. The large terrace offers views of either the pool or the Palm and as you soak up the vistas, it's hard to imagine a better spot for a day of lounging. The beachside beanbags area turns into a popular place to see and be seen on weekend evenings.

Map 1 C1 **Metro** Nakheel

Nawwara

Middle Eastern

JW Marriott Marquis Hotel,
  Business Bay, Zaa'beel   04 414 3000

A soft golden glow of candlelight greets you at this sublime setting. The feel is palatial without being intimidating – there's a vast lounge area where a DJ plays and cocktails are served post-dinner, an outdoor shisha terrace and an elegant dining area. You can opt for a mix of delicious mezze to share or a larger main – there are stacks of hot and cold dishes to choose from, including plenty of vegetarian options, and moreish desserts. Staff are friendly and properly educated about the dishes they serve. **Map** 2 A2 **Metro** Business Bay

Nina

Indian

Arabian Court At One&Only Royal Mirage,
  Al Sufouh 1   04 399 9999

Flickering candles and heavy velvet curtains set the scene at the One&Only's stylish Indo-European option, Nina. If hearty

curries and all-empowering fieriness is what you're after, you're
better off looking elsewhere – the food at Nina brings you on
an altogether more refined culinary journey to India. Think
subtle spiciness and refreshingly novel takes on Indian classics.
Amazing cocktails and Indian wine complete the dining
experience, along with a contemporary music soundtrack.
Map 3 C1 **Metro** Nakheel

Nineteen   European
The Address Montgomerie Dubai,
  Emirates Living, Al Thanyah 3   04 888 3444
The Montgomerie's flagship restaurant serves up rotisserie-
style food in chic surroundings and the show kitchen is loud
and proud. With views over the hotel's lush grounds, Nineteen
is a popular spot among local expats looking to indulge in the
restaurant's Friday brunch. For an even more relaxed – but no
less filling – affair, head here on a Saturday afternoon to tuck
into a beautifully satisfying traditional roast.
Map 3 B3 **Metro** Nakheel

Nobu   Japanese
Atlantis The Palm,
  Palm Jumeirah, Nakhlat Jumeira   04 426 2626
Nobuyuki Matsuhisa has upped the ante for sushi in the city.
Japanese food aficionados will love the exceptional quality,
attention to detail and huge menu of sushi, sashimi and
tempura, which is infused with subtle Arabian influences.
There's also a sake lounge to relax in after dinner. It's
recommended to book ahead. **Map** 1 C1 **Metro** Nakheel

The Observatory
International

Dubai Marriott Harbour Hotel & Suites,
Marsa Dubai
04 319 4795

It's all about the view at this atmospheric 52nd floor gastro-lounge. Spectacular 360° vistas over Dubai Marina and The Palm accompany the concise menu, while the cocktails are excellent. Arrive before sunset then stay for the evening to enjoy the panorama in full. **Map** 3 B1 **Metro** DAMAC

Okku
Japanese

The H Hotel Dubai, Trade Center 1
04 501 8777

There's more than enough to make you go 'mmm!' at Okku: the trendy decor, so very low lighting, great food and even greater, cocktail-fuelled party nights out. If prices are ever a sign of substance, then it definitely drives the point home, but its menu of sushi, sashimi and tempura is so fancifully executed that you may have to agree. Take the luxury up a notch and book one of the chic tatami rooms for private dining. Alternatively, just turn up at the weekend to sip cocktails in the bar. **Map** 2 E1 **Metro** World Trade Centre

Ossiano
Seafood

Atlantis The Palm, Palm Jumeirah, Nakhlat Jumeira 04 426 2626

Three Michelin-starred chef Santi Santamaria serves up Catalan-inspired simple, delicate seafood dishes at this impeccable eatery. Glistening chandeliers and floor-to-ceiling views of the enormous Ambassador Lagoon provides a formal, but romantic, setting to enjoy the seafood creations. **Map** 1 C1 **Metro** Nakheel

Okku

Pachanga
Hilton Dubai Jumeirah Resort, Marsa Dubai

Latin American
04 318 2530

Choose from the Havana-style bar, Brazilian barbecue, Mexican lounge or Argentinean terrace that surround the dancefloor at this hotspot. Start with fresh guacamole prepared at your table, then move onto the wide selection of mains: the seafood is delicious but the real winners are meat-eaters. Wednesday is tango night.

Map 3 A1 **Metro** Jumeirah Lakes Towers

Pai Thai
Al Qasr, Al Sufouh 1

Thai
04 366 6730

You'll have a night to remember at Pai Thai, from the abra ride to the restaurant to the novel Thai cuisine. If you are lucky, at some point in the evening you will be entertained by a traditionally dressed Thai dancer whose precise movements are as impressive as the food on your beautifully set table. The outdoor seating area is delightful and the menu provides the odd twist on familiar favourites.

Map 3 E1 **Metro** Mall of the Emirates

Pars Iranian Kitchen
Nr Chelsea Plaza Hotel, Al Jafiliya

Iranian
04 398 3107

Pars offers a traditional laid-back atmosphere a million miles from the modernity suggested by its neon sign. The menu includes a selection of grilled meats, kebabs and Iranian stews. Its delightful front garden, enclosed by a fairy light-entwined hedgerow, is home to low tables and soft, *majlis* bench seats. **Map** 1 H2 **Metro** Al Jafiliya

Pai Thai

Peppercrab   Singaporean
Grand Hyatt Dubai, Umm Hurair 1   04 317 2222

One of Dubai's many Asian restaurants, Peppercrab stands out thanks to its Singaporean theme. The noodles and chilli crab are authentic enough to make you feel like you're sitting in the middle of Clark's Quay in the Lion City. Also loyal to the fabulously tasty Singaporean cooking traditions, the menu's many Malay notes add welcome variety on your plate.

Map 4 B6 **Metro** Healthcare City

Pierchic   Seafood
Al Qasr, Al Sufouh 1   04 366 6730

Pierchic has arguably the best location of any Dubai restaurant. Perched at the end of a long wooden pier that juts into the Arabian Gulf, it affords front-row seats of an unobstructed Burj Al Arab, as well as Marsa Dubai and Palm Jumeirah in the distance. The delicately presented seafood and famed wine list come at a price but what you're really paying for is the view, especially if you request a table on the terrace. A good spot for romantic occasions.

Map 3 E1 **Metro** Mall of the Emirates

Ravi Restaurant   Pakistani
2nd December St, Al Satwa   04 331 5353

This much-loved diner offers a range of Pakistani curry favourites, rice dishes and freshly baked naan bread, alongside more adventurous fare such as fried brains. The setting is basic, but that hasn't stopped Ravi's from gaining cult status among local expats. Most people opt to sit outside

Peppercrab

with all of Satwa life on show, but dining is also available in the main restaurant or in the quieter family section. Either way, it's the food that really excels: you can eat like a king for under Dhs.30. **Map** 1 H2 **Metro** Al Jafiliya

Reem Al Bawadi
Arabic/Lebanese

Nr HSBC, Jumeira St, Jumeira 3 04 394 7444

Semi-isolated booths with thick Arabic cushions line the walls, while tables lined with armchairs fill the dark, bustling dining area. Reem Al Bawadi's mostly-Arab clientele is a good sign that the grills and mezze coming out of its kitchen are authentic. The Dubai Marina branch (04 452 2525) is a good choice for a similar experience in that end of town.
Map 1 G2 **Metro** Business Bay

Reflets Par Pierre Gagnaire

French

InterContinental Festival City Al Badia,
Al Kheeran

04 701 1127

From the Michelin-starred grandfather of molecular gastronomy, Pierre Gagnaire, comes a magical, imaginative and highly conceptual dining experience incorporating French cuisine. Bold purple carpet and pink chandeliers along with floor-to-ceiling mirrors and white tablecloths are the backdrop to a menu that strives to be a work of art. The romantic waterfront setting is the perfect place to sample wines from the specialist cellar. This is somewhere to go for that very special occasion. **Map** 1 J4 **Metro** Emirates

Signature By Sanjeev Kapoor

Indian

Melia Al Raffa

04 386 8111

The aptly named Signature, Sanjeev Kapoor's latest Dubai restaurant, bears all the hallmarks of its progressive and eclectic chef, with traditional Indian dishes given an innovative makeover. Samosas and bhajis take a back seat to such modern delights as tandoori wasabi lobster, basil pepper hammour tikka, honey mustard chicken chat puffs or paneer tikka with asparagus fritters and avocado mousse. Main courses continue the trend. It's traditional but with a twist – so expect to find paneer cooked in a butternut pumpkin and tomato sauce, goat shanks simmered in kashmiri and chilli onion gravy, and mutton cubes fried in pepper. Every inch the fine-dining restaurant, with elegant decor and a terrace for outdoor dining.
Map 2 K4 **Metro** ADCB

Ronda Locatelli

Ronda Locatelli
Italian

Atlantis The Palm, Palm Jumeirah, Nakhlat Jumeira   04 426 2626

An off-shoot of London's famed Locanda Locatelli, this restaurant features tables surrounding the centrepiece of the room: a huge stone-built wood-fired pizza oven. The casual menu offers a large selection of starters, pasta and mains, as well as a range of small dishes for sharing. Prices are quite reasonable for such a connected restaurant.

Map 1 C1 **Metro** Nakheel

Ruth's Chris Steak House
Steakhouse

The Address Dubai Marina, Marsa Dubai   04 454 9538

Ruth's Chris is an international institution among carnivores with a flair for fine fare, and the Dubai branch delivers on the high expectations. White leather sofas, red and dark panelling and slick service are topped off with superior steaks, served with a superb selection of accompaniments. A second branch is located at the Address hotel in Marsa Dubai (04 454 9538).

Map 2 E1 **Metro** World Trade Centre

Sahn Eddar
Afternoon Tea

Burj Al Arab, Umm Suqeim 3   04 301 7600

Those with normal-sized pockets won't get a better opportunity to inspect the Burj Al Arab. This is where you can slurp tea and nibble expensive scones at the base of the world's tallest atrium. There's an endless feast and a pot of your choice of the finest teas. After, consider a drink at the Skyview Bar for the stunning vistas 200m above the sea.

Map 3 E1 **Metro** Mall of the Emirates

Salmontini Le Resto

Seafood

Mall of the Emirates, Al Barsha 1

04 341 0222

Salmontini's chic interior is fashioned around large windows overlooking the mall's indoor ski slope. Choose from a selection of Scottish salmon, worked in every possible way (from smoked and grilled to cured and poached). All-inclusive deals offered during the week make a night here more cost-effective.

Map 3 E2 **Metro** Mall of the Emirates

Saravana Bhavan

Indian

Nr Karama Park, Al Karama

04 334 5252

This eatery takes its name from a much-loved hotel in Chennai, and here in Dubai, this unassuming joint is arguably the best of the area's south Indian restaurants. The menu is long enough to keep Indian expats interested but it's the thalis that draw crowds. For around Dhs.10 you can get a plate packed with colour and flavours, dal and chapatti. Fine Indian food doesn't come much cheaper or tastier.

Map 4 B3 **Metro** ADCB

Seafire Steakhouse & Bar

Steakhouse

Atlantis The Palm, Nakhlat Jumeira

04 426 2626

The warm colours at Seafire contrast nicely with the rest of Atlantis, while the smell of leather and cosy alcoves conspire to create the vibe of something well-established. Seafood and steak dominate the menu, all of it expertly prepared, and the signature dessert, a trio of chocolate treats, is worth waiting for, even if your waistline doth protest.

Map 1 C1 **Metro** Nakheel

Segreto

Italian

Souk Madinat Jumeirah, Al Sufouh 1   04 366 6730

Segreto is tucked away from the more bustling parts of Souk Madinat Jumeirah, and once inside, its smooth lines, pristine presentation and warm sandy tones give the experience a soothing start. Your dining journey can begin with sweet champagne cocktails and delicious breads. The food is aesthetically appealing, but the portions are more suited to a catwalk model than a prop forward.

Map 3 E1   **Metro** Mall of the Emirates

Shabestan

Persian

Radisson Blu Hotel, Dubai Deira Creek, Al Rigga   04 222 7171

This restaurant is as much about the decor as it is about the food. Ornate tables and chairs, decorative trinkets and traditional cooking stations combine to give a regal experience. The freshly baked breads epitomise the quality of food and the dishes are plentiful.

Map 4 D2   **Metro** Union

Shang Palace

Chinese

Shangri-La Hotel, Trade Center 1   04 405 2703

Shang Palace's food is delicious and the attentive staff are available to guide newcomers through the numerous options. Familiar dishes are well prepared, and set menus are available. With shark fin soup, live seafood and dim sum, this is certainly a place for something different. A well-stocked bar makes this a suitable venue to start an evening.

Map 2 C1   **Metro** Financial Centre

Toro Toro

Smiling BKK
Thai

Al Wasl Rd, Al Wasl
04 349 6677

This outstanding Thai pad near Safa Park is a rare thing: great food topped with good humour and superb service. The cheekily named dishes are reasonable at around Dhs.30, but with gossip mag pages for place mats and theme nights such as 'sing for your supper', it's the spirit that sets Smiling BKK apart. Check out its Facebook page for details of the hilarious menu. **Map** 1 G2 **Metro** Burj Khalifa/Dubai Mall

Splendido Restaurant
Italian

The Ritz-Carlton Dubai, Marsa Dubai
04 399 4000

Head to Splendido for an extensive menu featuring excellent, classic Italian fare with that 'just out of Italy' taste. Scrumptious mains and delicious desserts are all generously portioned, while the overall tone is quietly classy and pleasantly pleasing. There's also a good wine list with plenty of all-Italian favourites to delight discerning diners. To top it up, the hotel's enviable location on the JBR beach provides a great opportunity to take a casual stroll along the beach after your meal and walk off that pasta.

Map 3 A1 **Metro** DAMAC

Sultan's Lounge

Cafe

Jumeirah Zabeel Saray,
 Palm Jumeirah, Nakhlat Jumeira

04 453 0444

The interior section of Sultan's Lounge is finely appointed for a Turkish-themed hangout, but really the outlet is made by the large, relaxed terrace that is perfect for chilling out under the stars during the cooler months. Sandwiches and light bites dominate the menu, with the real immensity of variety reserved for the teas, coffees and other drinks. The lovely English or Ottoman afternoon teas are a must here.

Map 1 C2 **Metro** Nakheel

Sumibiya

Korean

Radisson Blu Hotel, Dubai Deira Creek,
 Al Rigga

04 222 7171

It's worth getting to know Korean cuisine, and eating is a social affair at this *yakiniku* (Korean grilled meat) eatery, where diners entertain themselves using the gas grill in the middle of every table, to sear, grill and charcoal bite-size morsels. It's informal, fun and tasty; if your food is overdone, you only have yourself to blame. **Map** 4 D2 **Metro** Union

Sur Mer (formerly Giannino)

Mediterranean

Meydan Beach, Marsa Dubai

04 433 3777

An offshoot of a Milanese dining institution by the same name, Giannino brings a slice of continental culinary tradition to JBR. Northern Italian classics grace the menu and while the beach club setting may not be as authentic as the original venue, this is certainly among your top choices when it comes to Italian food in this part of town.

Map 3 1A **Metro** Jumeirah Lakes Towers

Table 9

International

Hilton Dubai Creek, Al Rigga

04 212 7551

Located in the space that once held Gordon Ramsay's Verre restaurant, Table 9 is a British serving of fine dining; under the control of (highly experienced) new chef, Darren Velvick, since January 2014. The menu offers a mix of traditional favourites including chicken stuffed with foie gras and sea bass with egg, broccoli and hollandaise sauce. **Map** 4 D3 **Metro** Al Rigga

Tagine

Moroccan

The Palace At One&Only Royal Mirage, Al Sufouh 1

04 399 9999

Beneath ground level, through an enormous wooden door, past a *majlis* area draped in rich embroidery and perfumed with incense, you'll find the authentic Tagine. The low seating, arched alleys and courtyard setting, as well as the traditionally dressed waiters, create a traditional vibe as you sample the aromatic tagines and couscous creations.

Map 3 B1 **Metro** Nakheel

Taste of Fame
Sunset Mall, Jumeira 3

Italian/Asian
04 338 8552

A unique concept where diners are made to feel like A-list celebrities. Enter on a red carpet, get snapped by the paparazzi before dining alongside waxwork models of superstars and having your order taken by Spiderman. Food is a mix of Asian and Italian favourites.
Map 1 F2 **Metro** Business Bay

The Thai Kitchen
Park Hyatt Dubai, Port Saeed

Thai
04 317 2221

Intertwined around four live-cooking areas, Thai Kitchen is a slick, contemporary dining space. Thai food doesn't come fresher or more authentic on this side of Bangkok. With tapas-style portions at reasonable prices, your best bet is to order two or three per person and share. Finish it off by sipping a drink on the terrace with creek views; or pop over to The Terrace lounge next door.
Map 4 C5 **Metro** Deira City Centre

Thiptara
The Palace Downtown,
 Downtown Dubai, Burj Khalifa

Thai

04 888 3444

Expect fresh and spicy seafood at this quality Thai restaurant overlooking the Burj Khalifa and lake. There's a lively lobster tank from which to take your pick, while the wine list is extensive. This is a hard location to beat for impressing visitors and business associates.
Map 2 B3 **Metro** Burj Khalifa/Dubai Mall

Tokyo@thetowers
Japanese

Boulevard At Jumeirah Emirates Towers,
Trade Center 2
04 319 8088

With elegantly partitioned tatami rooms, lively teppanyaki tables and an eclectic menu, Tokyo@thetowers offers diners enough options to keep things interesting time after time. The private rooms all have traditional floor cushions, or you can choose to dine by the windows overlooking the mall.
Map 2 D2 **Metro** Emirates Towers

Toro Toro
Latin American

Grosvenor House, Marsa Dubai
04 399 8888

Entering the pan-Latin eatery is like stepping into a dramatic amphitheatre – giant bull sculptures flank the entrance and a two-storey fireplace lights the foyer. The menu is divided into three sections; from the sea, from the land and from the garden. Dishes are served tapas-style and each delicately prepared entree is served lovingly with influences from as far as Brazil to Peru. **Map** 3 B1 **Metro** DAMAC

Trader Vic's
Polynesian

Souk Madinat Jumeirah, Al Sufouh 1
04 366 5646

Try the delicious Asian-inspired dishes and moreish snacks or jump straight to the famously exotic cocktails, served in ceramic skulls and seashells. Many of the cocktails pack a serious, hidden kick – no wonder people love to dance here and the party keeps going until late! Head to the Crowne Plaza branch (04 305 6399) for live Cuban music every night.
Map 3 E1 **Metro** Mall of the Emirates

Traiteur
Park Hyatt Dubai, Port Saeed

French
04 317 2222

Having descended from an intimate bar via a dramatic staircase, you'll be struck by the restaurant's soaring ceilings. Traiteur's beautiful open kitchen then provides a great focal point for the French and modern European cuisine.
Map 4 C5 **Metro** Deira City Centre

Troyka
Ascot Hotel, Al Raffa

Russian
04 352 0900

Troyka's Russian-themed old world charm creates an intimate mood to enjoy the hearty, tasty cuisines on offer. The excellent-value Tuesday night buffet is all-inclusive and comprises time-honoured delicacies from the Russian kitchen. But food is not the only attraction here: if all you need is a dose of bizarre entertainment, a band plays every night from 10.30pm and a boisterous Vegas-style cabaret begins soon after.
Map 4 B2 **Metro** Al Fahidi

Villa Beach
Jumeirah Beach Hotel, Umm Suqeim 3

Mediterranean
04 406 8999

The buggy ride to the restaurant's door reveals the killer attraction: you're a bun's throw from the ocean and the Burj Al Arab. The beach-hut aesthetic has a Polynesian vibe but the food is mostly modern Mediterranean. The service is excellent, and although the scenery doesn't come cheap, the food is beautifully prepared and the wine list has been put together with care. **Map** 3 E1 **Metro** Mall of the Emirates

Wagamama

Al Fattan Marine Tower, JBR, Marsa Dubai

Japanese

04 399 5900

Perched above The Walk at JBR and modelled on a traditional Japanese ramen bar, with communal tables, Wagamama is good for a quick bite. Orders are freshly prepared; if you want to linger over your meal, it's wise to order a course at a time. Other branches are in Crowne Plaza (04 305 6060) and The Greens (04 361 5757). **Map** 3 A1 **Metro** DAMAC

West 14th New York Grill & Bar

Oceana Residences,
 The Trunk, Nakhlat Jumeira

Steakhouse

04 447 7601

It may be at the Oceana Beach Club but, make no mistake, West 14th is not the kind of place you turn up to in shorts and flip-flops. This Brooklyn-inspired, warehouse-style steakhouse is all about indulgence, from the comfy red leather armchairs to the oversized meat portions and the 12+ signature caipirinhas. **Map** 1 C1 **Metro** Nakheel

Yalumba

Le Meridien Dubai, Al Garhoud

International

04 702 2328

Famous for its raucous Friday bubbly buffets, this Australian-influenced restaurant doesn't limit itself to steak. Head there for the Thursday night buffet with unlimited champagne, sushi, stir-fry, seafood, steak and more desserts than you can possibly manage. Wednesdays feature an Aussie barbecue where you can even throw your own shrimps on. Just leave your board shorts at home.

Map 4 E6 **Metro** Airport Terminal 1

Yo! Sushi
Japanese

Dubai Marina Mall, Marsa Dubai
04 399 7708

This bright and cheerful chain specialises in serving up sushi and other unashamedly stereotypical Japanese bites in a fun setting. The Marina branch is no exception; grab a table at the bar to sample the small portions transported around on a conveyor belt. Elsewhere in the city, other branches include DIFC (04 363 7404) and Mirdif (04 284 3995).

Map 3 A1 **Metro** Jumeirah Lakes Towers

Zafran
Indian

Dubai Marina Mall, Marsa Dubai
04 399 7357

As far as mall-eats go, Zafran stands apart – Michelin-starred chef Atul Kochars is behind the venture and you can look forward to some superbly tasty Indian creations. There's another branch in Mirdif City Centre (04 284 0987).

Map 3 A1 **Metro** Jumeirah Lakes Towers

Zheng He's
Chinese

Mina A'Salam, Al Sufouh 1
04 366 6730

Zheng He's superb take on Chinese delicacies, together with the restaurant's exquisite waterside spot in Souk Madinat Jumeirah, ensure a constant stream of patrons. The dim sum and mini-roll starters are divine, while the marinated fish, stir-fried style meat and duck are all worth discovering as well. The wine list is as thick as it is pricey, but in terms of culinary experience you certainly get what you pay for. It's the perfect way to end a day browsing the Souk Madinat.

Map 3 E2 **Metro** Mall of the Emirates

Zheng He's

Zuma

Japanese

Dubai International Financial Centre (DIFC),
Trade Center 2   04 425 5660

Since its opening, Zuma has gained a firm following as one of
Dubai's best restaurants. The stunning space is elegantly lit,
with clean lines of wood and glass to set the scene. The food
that arrives from the open kitchen and sushi bar is presented
in classic Japanese style – it is all about simplicity and flair
here, with prices to match. If dinner is beyond your budget,
opt for a drink at the bar. **Map** 2 C2 **Metro** Emirates Towers

Bars, Pubs & Clubs

Sky-high cocktail lounges, beachside bars and enough clubs to keep you dancing for a year all jostle for your evening attention.

360°
Bar

Jumeirah Beach Hotel, Umm Suqeim 3   04 406 8999

One visit to this Umm Suqeim hottie is enough to convince you that this is what holidays were made for: like a static carousel for grown-ups, 360° is a circular rooftop with a bar at its heart. The place boasts stunning panoramic views of the Arabian Gulf. Early arrivals (it opens at 5pm, and 4pm on Friday) can take their pick of low white couches and suck whichever colourful shisha they fancy. Sunset signals cocktails, beats and one of the city's best alfresco nights.

Map 3 E1   **Metro** Mall of the Emirates

The Agency
Bar

Souk Madinat Jumeirah, Al Sufouh 1   04 366 6730

With a veritable vineyard of the squashed grape on offer, even wine connoisseurs won't fail to find something quaffable on the 30 page wine menu. Dark wood, exposed brickwork and perch-friendly seating complete the chic setting. Tasty tapas-style bites include spring rolls, spicy prawns and delicious olives. There's another branch in Emirates Towers which has a more extensive food menu.

Map 3 E1   **Metro** Mall of the Emirates

360°

Bahri Bar

Bar

Mina A'Salam, Al Sufouh 2   04 366 6730

Imagine you had the chance to design the perfect bar. For starters you'd include a stunning view, with windtower rooftops, rustling palm trees, meandering canals, the towering Burj Al Arab and sparkling ocean beyond. The bar could have rich furnishings, comfortable seating and ornately engraved lanterns. On the menu you'd make sure a comprehensive cocktail selection was accompanied by wines, beers, and delicious nibbles. Welcome to Bahri Bar.

Map 3 E1 **Metro** Mall of the Emirates

Going Out

Restaurants & Cafes

Bar 44
Bar

Grosvenor House, Marsa Dubai   04 399 8888

At Bar 44 waiters with waistcoats that match the bar's carpets whizz around with expensive bottles of champagne, a jazz singer swoons impressively at a grand piano, and plumes of (pricey) cigar smoke fill the air. The cocktails are equally regal and you get to enjoy it all to a backdrop of some great marina views. **Map** 3 B1 **Metro** DAMAC

Barasti
Bar

Le Meridien Mina Seyahi Beach Resort &
 Marina, Al Sufouh 1   04 399 3333

Barasti is a Dubai nightlife institution. The sprawling beachside venue features inviting loungers and daybeds, a downstairs bar and big screens for the all-important events on the sporting scene, along with heaps of casual charm and plenty of revelling party-goers. This laid-back bar is a firm expat favourite, loved for its meaty menu, jugs of Pimms and panoramic vistas, not to mention the fact you can turn up in flip-flops or Friday finery depending on your mood.
Map 3 B1 **Metro** DAMAC

Barzar
Bar

Souk Madinat Jumeirah, Al Sufouh 2   04 366 6730

The upper level of this slick two-floor bar is open in the middle so you can peer over at the band and drinkers below. The overall vibe is relaxed and urban, complete with eclectic drinks such as beer cocktails (champagne with Guinness) and traditional long drinks. **Map** 3 E1 **Metro** Mall of the Emirates

Belgian Beer Cafe

Pub

Crowne Plaza Dubai Festival City, Al Kheeran   04 701 1127

Aside from the namesake beverage, the main draws are
the *moules frites*; mussels served in your choice of sauce
with crisp fries and lots of bread for mopping up the juices.
Fittingly for a Belgian joint, the beer selection is top notch, if a
tad on the expensive side. The traditional dining room fills up
fast, as does the terrace, and the views are second to none.

Map 1 J4 **Metro** Emirates

Bidi Bondi

Bar

Clubhouse Al Manhal, Shoreline Apartments,
 Palm Jumeirah, Nakhlat Jumeira   04 427 0515

This laid-back offering on Palm Jumeirah offers indoor and
alfresco space, with a beach diner and Aussie-style hangout
lounge. There is a great range of mocktails, cocktails, beers
and wines to choose from, and, should you get hungry, the
food menu offers hefty burgers, sandwiches and salads plus
bar snacks. Breakfast is also available for the morning after.

Map 3 C1 **Metro** Nakheel

Blends

Bar

The Address Dubai Marina, Marsa Dubai   04 436 7777

Blends is a popular hangout among Marsa Dubai locals
looking for a night out on the town. Arrive early to secure one
of the plush armchairs before revelling party-goers take over
the small dancefloor area. An extensive drinks list lubricates
the atmosphere and there's a separate cigar lounge.

Map 3 A1 **Metro** DAMAC

Blue Bar

Bar

Novotel World Trade Centre, Trade Center 2   04 332 0000

Jazz fans unite for some of the best live music in town. Hidden at the back of the Novotel, the Blue Bar has a relaxed, low-key vibe with enough 'it' factor to give it street cred but without any delusions of grandeur. You can opt to either pull up a stool at the large square bar, or get cosy on one of the leather sofas and armchairs.

Map 2 E2 **Metro** World Trade Centre

Boudoir

Nightclub

Dubai Marine Beach Resort & Spa, Jumeira 1   04 345 5995

This exclusive spot can be as difficult to get into as a lady's chamber but once you get past the doormen – as long as you are appropriately dressed – you will be treated to a Parisian-style club that's perfect for dangerous liaisons. The regular free drinks for ladies help pack the circular dancefloor.

Map 1 H2 **Metro** World Trade Centre

Buddha Bar

Bar

Grosvenor House, Marsa Dubai   04 317 6000

Buddha Bar has the wow factor. From the entrance, a seductively lit corridor leads you past private lounges and tucked-away alcoves; all perfectly decadent places to dine, lounge, and socialise. With the Buddha Bar's famous mix of music, some of the best cocktails in town and a selection of tasty Asian treats, this Grosvenor House haunt is a firm favourite among Dubai's army of socialites.

Map 3 B1 **Metro** DAMAC

Clockwise from top left: Double Decker, Barzar, Cavalli Club

Calabar

Bar

The Address Downtown Dubai, Burj Khalifa   04 436 8888

A large, sweeping bar serving cigars and all manner of drinks from international brews to Latin cocktails is the centrepiece of this chic lounge. There's also a decent selection of nibbles and the terrace offers spectacular views of the Burj Khalifa.
Map 2 B3 **Metro** Burj Khalifa/Dubai Mall

Caramel Restaurant & Lounge

Bar

Dubai International Financial Centre (DIFC),
 Zaa'beel 2   04 425 6677

This is a place where those who work hard come to play in a similar manner. Oozing urban cool, the stylish restaurant spills out from the bar through open walls on to the terrace, where cabanas set the mood for stylish lounging. In addition to an extensive selection of drinks, there's a menu of light bites and nibbles to keep hunger at bay. During the day, Caramel turns into one of the more stylish spots for lunch around DIFC.
Map 2 C2 **Metro** Financial Centre

Cavalli Club

Nightclub

Fairmont Dubai, Trade Center 1   04 332 9260

Roberto Cavalli's leopard print and Swarovski encrusted nightspot is one of the city's places to be seen if you're part of the 'it' crowd. It's all suitably decadent and as unashamedly over the top as can be expected from the Italian designer. There's also a cocktail and cigar lounge, wine bar and even a boutique shop to enjoy – if you can get through the door.
Map 2 E1 **Metro** World Trade Centre

Chi@The Lodge

Nightclub

Al Nasr Leisureland, Oud Metha

04 337 9470

The Lodge is always busy with its indoor and outdoor dancefloors, lots of seating and large screens and VIP cabanas. The regular theme nights with fancy dress are popular, especially the legendary 'cheese'. On top of all that, it's easy to get taxis outside, there's often a shawarma stand in the car park and entrance is free before 10pm on most nights.

Map 4 B4 **Metro** Oud Metha

Dhow & Anchor

Pub

Jumeirah Beach Hotel, Umm Suqeim 3

04 406 8999

Dhow & Anchor's bar is a popular spot, particularly during happy hour and sporting events – try the outdoor terrace if you are dining and enjoy glimpses of the Burj Al Arab. The menu includes the usual range of drinks and terrific curries, roast dinners, pies, and fish and chips.

Map 3 E1 **Metro** Mall of the Emirates

Double Decker

Pub

Al Murooj Rotana, Trade Center 2

04 321 1111

On a Friday afternoon this could be your average pub in just any town around the world. With big screen sports, dangerously long happy hours and karaoke, many appreciate the relative charms this pub provides. Fridays are the most crowded thanks to the inexpensive boozy brunch. Somewhat refreshingly, there is little need to worry about dress code; trainers, flip-flops and shorts are all fine.

Map 2 C2 **Metro** Financial Centre

Eclipse Bar

Bar

InterContinental Dubai Festival City, Al Kheeran   04 701 1127

On the 26th floor, Eclipse is all about glamour, with red leather padded walls, marble tables and a huge bar serving hundreds of different cocktails. It's also a great vantage point for cityscape views of Sheikh Zayed Road's high-rises.

Map 1 J4 **Metro** Emirates

Embassy Dubai

Nightclub

Grosvenor House, Marsa Dubai   04 317 6000

In addition to a club and restaurant, this Grosvenor House venue boasts a vodka and champagne bar. The decor is opulent: intricately tiled walls, baroque lamps, candlelit tables and floor-to-ceiling windows overlooking the Marsa Dubai skyline all add to the luxurious feel to make a decadent night out. **Map** 3 B1 **Metro** DAMAC

Healey's Bar & Terrace

Bar

Bonnington Jumeirah Lakes Towers,
 Jumeirah Lakes Towers, Al Thanyah 5   04 356 0600

Wednesday night is the night at Healey's, which has a live DJ and three free drinks for women from 10pm to 11pm. The stylish bar, with an ultra-chic glass bar, is perfect for glam patrons looking for a place to start the evening. Prop up at the bar and you can almost believe you are sipping cocktails in a Manhattan bar, and not in the middle of Jumeirah Lakes Towers. To top off the drama, head to the terrace, where you can sip cocktails outside surrounded by marina vistas.

Map 3 A2 **Metro** Jumeirah Lakes Towers

Top: The Irish Village, Bottom: Healey's Bar & Terrace

The Hub
Bar

Sofitel Dubai Jumeirah Beach, Marsa Dubai   04 448 4848

A cut above your average sports bar, The Hub, located in the Sofitel hotel, is a welcome addition to the JBR Walk. Ascend above the crowds and get ready to sample a decent selection of bottled and draught beers. Flat screen TVs show an array of sports and the buzzing atmosphere makes it a popular hangout. **Map** 3 A1 **Metro** Jumeirah Lakes Towers

The Irish Village
Pub

Nr Dubai Tennis Stadium, Al Garhoud   04 282 4750

The Irish Village is the nearest thing Dubai has to a beer garden, and the best place to go for fish and chips (complete with Guinness batter) and a pint of the dark stuff. Despite being one of the largest pubs in the city, this award-winning haunt is almost always packed with people looking to let their hair down while enjoying a bit of home nostalgia. Expect hearty pub food, twinkling lights in the trees and a live musician or two. **Map** 4 D6 **Metro** GGICO

Jetty Lounge
Bar

One&Only Royal Mirage, Al Sufouh 1   04 399 9999

This beachside bar manages to strike a great balance between stylish and relaxed. Located in the exclusive One&Only Royal Mirage, just steps from the hotel's private beach, the loungy setting is perfect for sundowners: plop onto comfy seats, kick back and indulge in tasty snacks. You can also take a ferry to the hotel's sister property, One&Only The Palm. **Map** 3 B1 **Metro** Nakheel

N'Dulge Nightclub
Nightclub

Atlantis The Palm,
 Palm Jumeirah, Nakhlat Jumeira   04 426 0561

Expect something special from Atlantis, like a suspended
catwalk in a nightclub – because that's what you get at
N'Dulge, along with lashings of cool. This space is modern,
glam and packed with dedicated clubbers looking to let their
hair down in style. **Map** 1 C1 **Metro** Nakheel

Neos
Bar

The Address Downtown Dubai,   04 436 8927
 Downtown Dubai, Burj Khalifa

Dubai is not short of bars with the wow-factor and Neos
definitely falls into this lofty bracket: take the lift to the 63rd
floor and get ready to be wowed by the views. With huge
wall-to-wall windows, Neos' staggering height makes it
hard to play it cool as you stare out at Burj Khalifa and the
city beyond. You'll feel like a star.
Map 2 B3 **Metro** Burj Khalifa/Dubai Mall

Nezesaussi Grill
Bar

Al Manzil Hotel, Downtown Dubai, Burj Khalifa   04 428 5888

This upmarket sports bar, home to the best ribs in town, has
enough glam to keep women happy while the match is on.
Tastefully decked out in memorabilia, Nezesaussi might be a
tongue-twister but once you've been there, the name is hard
to forget. Although it boasts South African sausages, lamb
from New Zealand and Australian steaks, it's not all beer and
beef. **Map** 2 B3 **Metro** Burj Khalifa/Dubai Mall

Oeno Wine Bar
Bar

The Westin Dubai Mina Seyahi Beach Resort &
  Marina, Al Sufouh 1   04 399 4141

Oeno's decor is modern and stylish, and the wine wall,
complete with a librarian-style bookshelf ladder, adds a sense
of decadence. There's a temperature-controlled cheese room
with over 50 types of cheese, as well as a menu full of antipasti
options. For an unbeatable date, book a table on the terrace.
Map 3 B1 **Metro** Nakheel

The Rooftop Terrace & Sports Lounge
Bar

One&Only Royal Mirage, Al Sufouh 1   04 399 9999

Clever design and lighting combine with a subtle DJ to make
this one of Dubai's finest bars. Rooftop has a superb view
of Palm Jumeirah, Moroccan decor with comfy *majlis*-style
seating, intimate booths with huge cushions and a good
menu of cocktails and bottled beers. If you're looking to kick
back and relax under the stars there's no better place.
Map 3 B1 **Metro** Nakheel

Sanctuary Pool Bar & Lounge
Bar

Sheraton Dubai Mall of the Emirates,
  Al Barsha 1   04 377 2000

Head to Sanctuary's lofty poolside during the day to enjoy
relaxed light bites and cocktails with a storming view of
Marsa Dubai, The Palm and Jumeira as a fitting backdrop
while you soak up some rays. By night, Sanctuary has more
of a chilled lounge ambience, serving up simple cuisine and
cocktails. **Map** 3 E2 **Metro** Mall of the Emirates

Shades
Bar

The Address Dubai Marina, Marsa Dubai   04 436 7777

Located on the fourth floor of The Address Dubai Marina, Shades features white comfy sofas, making the pristine lounge a perfect hangout for pre-dinner drinks or shisha, although you can also tuck into BBQ fare here.

Map 3 A1 **Metro** DAMAC

Siddharta Lounge By Buddha Bar
Bar

Grosvenor House, Marsa Dubai   04 317 6000

Ample lashings of plush white seating, gold accents and glam marble finishing set the scene at Siddharta. You'll be spoiled for choice with a posh snack menu that features a mouthwatering selection of Asian-Mediterranean specialities, including Wagyu beef mini burgers with orange soy and crispy prawn spring rolls with tamarind dipping sauce. There are also larger mains if you fancy a proper sit-down dinner. Drinks aren't cheap, but this is a place to be seen.

Map 3 B1 **Metro** DAMAC

Sho Cho
Bar

Dubai Marine Beach Resort & Spa, Jumeira 1   04 346 1111

Sho Cho is a perfectly fine Japanese restaurant but that's not the real reason the beautiful set flock to its shoreline location. The sizeable bar, flanked by two alfresco eating areas and guarded by sharp-eyed waiters, is the real attraction. The tiny dancefloor is a poser's paradise; there's barely room to swing a man in tight jeans.

Map 1 H2 **Metro** World Trade Centre

Skyview Bar
Burj Al Arab, Umm Suqeim 3

Bar

04 301 7600

Come here in the evening for high-class cocktails and stunning views. Alternately, come for the afternoon tea and sit back, savouring the view while a waiter piles vast quantities of finger sandwiches, mini buns, cakes and biscuits on to your table, accompanied by a pot of tea and a glass of champagne. Book well in advance.

Map 3 E1 **Metro** Mall of the Emirates

Trader Vic's Mai-Tai Lounge
Al Fattan Marine Tower, JBR, Marsa Dubai

Bar

04 399 8993

Perched above JBR Walk in Marsa Dubai, this large bar is faithful to the iconic Trader Vic's style: decked out in Polynesian fixtures and fittings, Mai-Tai serves tropical cocktails, accompanied by tasty, if expensive, bar snacks. The spacious dancefloor provides a clubby feel should the cocktails put you in the mood to take a spin.

Map 3 A1 **Metro** Jumeirah Lakes Towers

The Terrace
Park Hyatt Dubai, Port Saeed

Bar

04 317 2222

Sweep through the Park Hyatt's atmospheric grounds and greenery, and you'll reach The Terrace: a haven of unhurried vibes and chillout tunes by the creek. Awash with contemporary white, chrome and wood, the interior extends out through shiny conservatory doors to an awning-adorned terrace. Scattered with couches and wooden tables, it's a gorgeous alfresco spot by the water. As far as chilled out

Uptown Bar

terraces go, this is easily one of the most exclusive venues for sundowners in town. **Map** 4 C5 **Metro** Deira City Centre

The Underground Pub
Pub

Habtoor Grand Beach Resort & Spa,
 Marsa Dubai   04 408 4221

Themed on the London Tube, this small and compact space quickly fills up during popular sporting events, there are screens showing live sports, a dartboard and pool tables, as well as light bites and burgers. **Map** 3 B1 **Metro** DAMAC

Uptown Bar

Bar

Jumeirah Beach Hotel, Umm Suqeim 3   04 406 8999

Take the lift to the 24th floor to find this small but perfectly formed bar. The cool interior is classy enough, but Uptown's selling point is the outdoor terrace: it's a perfect spot for 'sunset behind the Burj' photo ops. Get there at 6pm to take advantage of the half-price happy hour and cute little canapes. **Map** 3 E1 **Metro** Mall of the Emirates

Voda Bar

Bar

Jumeirah Zabeel Saray,
 Palm Jumeirah, Nakhlat Jumeira   04 453 0444

It's a bit of a trek to the outer fringes of The Palm, but if Japanese nibbles and exotic cocktails tickle your fancy, a cab ride to this sushi bar is well worth it. Located in the extravagant Jumeirah Zabeel Saray hotel, Voda Bar has a 15 page list of Japanese-inspired cocktails – including the refreshing Sake Highball – to sample over a platter of light bites from the land of the rising sun. **Map** 1 C2 **Metro** Nakheel

Warehouse

Bar

Le Meridien Dubai, Al Garhoud   04 702 2560

Warehouse's ground floor contains both an impressively stocked beer bar and well-rounded wine bar. Up the spiral staircase is a dual-personality restaurant – half fine dining and half sushi – where the food is elegantly displayed. As if that weren't enough, there's a vodka bar and a lounge club with an intimate dancefloor, DJ booth and just enough flash to warrant dressing up. **Map** 4 E6 **Metro** Airport Terminal 1

Wavebreaker
Bar

Hilton Dubai Jumeirah Resort, Marsa Dubai   04 399 1111

This popular beach bar at the Hilton Jumeirah is the perfect place to spend a laidback afternoon by the sea; grab a drink and order a plate of nibbles to share while watching the sun go down. Later, the alfresco joint turns into an evening hangout with music, billiards and shisha.

Map 3 A1 **Metro** Jumeirah Lakes Tower

XL Beach Club
Nightclub

Habtoor Grand Beach Resort & Spa,
 Marsa Dubai   04 399 5000

With ample style and more than a pinch of decadence, XL Beach Club lives up to its grandiose name. Private cabanas (available to hire for an eyebrow-raising fee) and a shimmering pool set the scene, superstar DJs regularly spin the discs here and, once darkness falls, the chic outdoors venue plays host to some of the best parties in town.

Map 3 B1 **Metro** Nakheel

Zinc
Nightclub

Crowne Plaza Dubai, Trade Center 1   04 331 1111

A slinky superclub experience awaits at Zinc: the soundtrack is modern R&B, house and hip-hop, with Housexy (Ministry of Sound) and Kinky Malinki ferrying over of UK DJs. Design-wise there are shiny flatscreens, lounge areas and glitzy mirrored walls, as well as a big dancefloor and mammoth bar. All combined, every night is a party night at this Crowne Plaza haunt. **Map** 2 D1 **Metro** Emirates Towers

Index

#

1847	167
360°	300
4WDs	164

A

Abaya	15
Abra	63
Absolute Adventure	142
Abu Dhabi	130
Abu Dhabi Desert Challenge	52, 152, 162, 164
Abu Dhabi Golf Club	164
Abu Dhabi Grand Prix	53, 165
Abu Dhabi HSBC Golf Championship	164
Accidents & Emergencies	45
Act, The	228
Address Downtown Dubai, The	66
Address Montgomerie, The	226
Aerogulf Services	140, 142
Agency, The	300
Ahasees Spa & Club	167
Air Arabia	37
Air France	37
Airlines	37
American Airlines	37
Airport	75
Airport Transfer	37
Ajman	136
Ajman Kempinski Hotel & Resort	136
Akaru Spa	167
Al Ahmadiya School & Heritage House	92
Al Ain	132, 133
Al Ain Aerobatic Show	164
Al Ain Palace Museum	133
Al Ain Zoo	133
Al Badia Golf Club	149
Al Boom Diving	159
Al Boom Tourist Village	148
Al Bustan Rotana	75
Al Dawaar	92, 247
Al Fahidi Historical Neighbourhood	78, 84, 85, 86, 89, 184
Al Fahidi Street	192
Al Fanar	109, 225
Al Fanar Restaurant & Cafe	247
Al Khayma	247
Al Maha Desert Resort & Spa	76
Al Mahara	117, 248
Al Maktoum International Airport	18
Al Mallah	248
Al Mamzar	92
Al Muntaha	248
Al Nafoorah	249
Al Nasr Square	90
Al Qasr	118
Al Sarab Rooftop Lounge	76
Al Shindagha	84
Al Sufouh	116
Al Wasl Road	216
Alpha Tours	142
Alserkal Avenue	33
Amara Spa	107, 168
Ambassador Lagoon	280
American Hospital	
...ADVERT	xi
Amphitheatre	123
Angsana Spa & Health Club	168
Antique Museum, The	217
AOC	250
Après	121, 250

Aprons & Hammers	250	
Aquara	105, 251	
Aquaventure	34, 117	
Arabesque Cafe	251	
Arabian Adventures	142	
Arabian Ranches Golf Club	149	
Arabian Tea House	251	
Arabic	42	
Armani Cafe	32	
Armani hotel	96	
Armani Hotel Dubai	66	
Armani/Amal	252	
Armani/Peck	252	
Art	184	
Art Source	184	
Asado	252	
Ascott Park Place Dubai	66	
Asha's	253	
Ashiana	253	
At The Top, Burj Khalifa	21, 96	
At.mosphere	21, 96, 253	
Atlantis The Palm	30, 56, 67, 117	
Audi Driving Skills	152	
Automatic	254	
Aviation Club, The	107	
Avis	58	
Ayurvedic	168	
AZ.U.R	254	

B

B/Attitude Spa	168	
Bab Al Shams Desert		
Resort & Spa	76	
Bahri Bar	301	
Balloon Adventures	140, 142	
Balloon ride	140	
Bamboo Lagoon	256	
Banana Boats	158	
Bar 44	302	

Barasti	34, 116, 302	
Bargaining	182	
Bars	300	
Barzar	302	
Bastakiah Nights	225, 256	
Beach Bar & Grill	257	
Beach Centre	192	
Beach Resort & Marina	71	
Beachcombers	257	
Belgian Beer Cafe	106, 303	
BiCE Mare	257	
Bidi Bondi	303	
Big Bus Tours	26, 140, 142	
Big Red sand dune	135	
Blends	303	
Bloomingdale's	202, 213	
Blue Bar	304	
Blue Elephant	258	
Blue Flame	258	
Blue Souk	137	
Boardwalk	107, 258	
Boudoir	304	
Boulevard, The	98	
Boulevard, The		
at Emirates Towers	32, 167	
Bowling alley	206, 208	
Bristol Middle East		
Yacht Solutions	142	
British Airways	37	
Brunch	221	
Buddha Bar	168, 304	
Budget Rent A Car	58	
Buhairah Corniche	137	
Bur Dubai	24, 192	
Burj Al Arab	25, 34, 67, 117, 176	
Burj Khalifa	18, 25, 34, 72, 96, 98	
Burj Khalifa Lake	204	
BurJuman	198	
Bus	57, 56	

Bussola	258, 260	
Butcher Shop & Grill, The	260	

C

Cable Car	122	
Cafe Arabesque	260	
Cafes	246	
Calabar	306	
Camel Racing	53, 160	
Camel Ride	23, 105, 160	
Car Rental Agencies	58, 60	
Caramel Restaurant		
& Lounge	306	
Carpets	185	
Cavalli Club	72, 306	
Center Cut	261	
Center For Cultural		
Understanding	86	
Central Souk	137	
Century Village	107	
Chef Lanka	194	
Chi@The Lodge	34, 307	
Children's City	122	
China Club, The	261	
Cinema	226	
Cleopatra's Spa		
& Wellness	170	
Climate	40	
Clubs	300	
Comedy	227	
Counter Culture	261	
Courtyard, The	217	
Creek Park	58, 74, 93, 122	
Creekside Souks	93	
Crime & Safety	44	
Culture & Heritage	6, 10	
Currency	41	
Customs	38	
Cycling	58	

Day Cruise 148
De La Mer Day Spa 170
Debenhams 212
Deira 24, 33, 84, 90, 192
Deira City Centre 200
Desert Adventures 142
Desert Challenge 164
Desert Rangers 134, 142
Desert Resort 76
Desert Safari 140
Dhow & Anchor 307
Dhow Charters 148
Diamondlease Car Rental 58
Dibba 134
Disabilities 45
Diving 156
Dolphin Bay 117
Dolphins 93, 134, 148
Double Decker 307
Downtown &
   Sheikh Zayed Road 96
DP World Tour
   Championship 53, 161
Drakkar Noir 1000
   Dunes Rally 152
Drink Driving 45
Driving & Car Hire 58
Dubai Aquarium 32
   ...ADVERT 203
Dubai Aquarium &
   Underwater Zoo 97
Dubai Autodrome 32, 152, 162
Dubai Community
   Theatre & Arts Centre 205, 228
Dubai Creek Golf
   & Yacht Club 107, 150
Dubai Deira Creek 75
Dubai Designer Market 191

Dubai Dolphinarium 93
   ...ADVERT vi, vii
Dubai Duty Free Tennis
   Championships 51, 107
Dubai Ferry 63
Dubai Festival City 67, 149, 200
Dubai Flea Market 191
Dubai Fountain 29, 98
Dubai International
   Airport 18, 36
Dubai International
   Art Centre 111
Dubai International
   Film Festival 53, 226
Dubai Mall, The 27, 29, 72, 96,
   99, 154, 202
Dubai Marina 34, 168
Dubai Marina Mall 191, 201
Dubai Marriott Harbour
   Hotel & Suites 74
Dubai Metro 54
Dubai Museum 33, 85, 188
Dubai Outlet Mall 204
Dubai Polo &
   Equestrian Club 226
Dubai Racing Club 162
Dubai Rugby Sevens 163
Dubai Shopping Festival 51
Dubai Sound City 107
Dubai Sports City 18
Dubai Tennis Stadium 107
Dubai Tourism &
   Travel Services 142
Dubai Transport 46
Dubai World Central - Al
   Maktoum International
   Airport 36
Dubai World Cup 18, 52, 162
Dubai Youth Hostel 75

Ductac 228
Dune Bashing 32, 156
Dusit Thani 72

E

East Coast 133
Eauzone 262
Eclipse Bar 308
Eid Al Adha 50
Eid Al Fitr 50
El Malecon 115, 262
Electricity & Water 40
Electronics Souk 192
Els Club Dubai, The 150
Embassy Suites 308
Emirates Airline 37
Emirates Airline Dubai
   Rugby Sevens 163,53
Emirates Golf Club 150
Emirates Motor
   Sports Federation 152
Emirates Palace 132
Emirates Towers Hotel 98
Emirati Cuisine 85
Etihad Airways 37
EuroStar Rent A Car 58
Events 51
Exchange Grill, The 263

F

Fabindia 215
Fairmont Dubai 72
Fakhreldine 264
Farm, The 264
Favourite Things
   Mother and Child 202
Federation Rally 152
Ferrari World Abu Dhabi 132, 152
   ...ADVERT 131

Festival City	106
Festival Mall	200
Festival Waterfront	
Centre	109, 200
FIA GT Championships	154
Fire & Ice	264
Fish Market	24, 266
Fish Souk	93
Flavours On Two	266
flydubai	37
Food & Drink	10
Formation of the UAE	8
Formula 1	
Etihad Airways	53, 165
Fortress	135
Forts	138
Fountain Restaurant	266
Fujairah	134, 158

G

Galleries	184
Gallery	127
Gallery 76	111
Gallery Isabelle Van	
Den Eynde	126
Gallery One	196, 217
Gardens	122
Garhoud	106
Gaucho	267
Getting Around	54
Ghalilah	137
Gifts	194
Ginger & Lace	210
Glasshouse Brasserie	75, 267
Global Village	126
Gold & Diamond Park	216
Gold Souk	24, 93, 192, 216
Golden Tulip	
Khasab Hotel Resort	134

Golf	146, 149
Golf Academy	150
Grand Prix	53, 165
Grosvenor House Dubai	68
Growing Trade	8
Guesthouses & Hostels	75
Gulf Air	37
Gulf Ventures	142
...ADVERT	143

H

Habtoor Grand Resort	156
Hajar Mountains	134, 135, 140
Hakkasan	267
Hammams	166
Harry Ghatto's	98
Hatta	32, 135
Hatta Fort Hotel	135
Hatta Pools	135
Hawthorn Suites	
by Wyndham	68
...ADVERT	65
Healey's Bar & Terrace	308
Heavenly Spa By Westin	
Dubai Mina Seyahi	171
Heritage & Diving Villages	85
Heritage Village	135
Hertz UAE	58
Hilton Dubai Creek	75
Hilton Dubai	
Jumeirah Resort	68
Hofbräuhaus	268
Holidays	50
Hong Loong	268
Horse Racing	162
Horse Riding	77
Hot Air Ballooning	151
Hotel, XVA Art	75
Hotels	64

Hub, The	310
Hypermarkets	214

I

Ibn Battuta Mall	204
Ice Skating Rink	154, 202
ICHO	268
IMAX	205
Imperium	270
Independent &	
Noteworthy Shops	215
Iranian Mosque	127
Irish Village	106, 310
Islam	6
Ivy, The	270
iZ	270

J

JA Jebel Ali	
Golf Resort	77, 151
Jamie's Italian	271
jamjar, the	127, 33
Jashanmal	213
Jazz Festival	52
JBR Beach	102
Jeep Jamboree	152
Jetty Lounge	310
Jewellery	194
Jogging Track	123
Jumeira	110, 115
Jumeirah Beach Hotel	68
Jumeirah Beach Park	31, 111
Jumeirah	
Beach Residence	201, 246
Jumeirah Beach Road	192
Jumeirah Emirates Towers	72, 98
Jumeirah Golf Estates	161
Jumeirah	
Mosque	15, 22, 110, 111

Jumeirah Open Beach 110, 112
Jumeirah Zabeel Saray 270
JW's Steakhouse 271

K

Karama 128, 223
Karama Complex 193
Karat 271
Kartdrome 154
Karting 32
Kayaking 158
Kempinski Hotel
  Mall Of The Emirates 72
Khalid Lagoon 137
Khan Murjan 185, 194, 210
Khasab Travel & Tours 148
Khazana 272
Khor Fakkan 134
Khor Kalba 134
Kids Connection 210
KidZania 202
  ...ADVERT 153
Kitesurfing 146
KLM Royal Dutch Airlines 37
Knight Tours 142
Kosebasi 272

L

La Brasserie 272
La Petite Maison 273
Lamcy Plaza 122
Language 42
Laughter Factory, The 227
Le Meridien
  Al Aqah Beach Resort 134
Le Meridien Dubai 75
Le Meridien
  Mina Seyahi 116, 156
Le Royal Meridien Beach 69

Leap of Faith 117
Levantine 273
Lime Tree Cafe &
  Kitchen, The 273
Live Music 227
Lobby Lounge 274
Long Yin 274
Lost Chambers
  Aquarium 30, 117
Luciano's 274
Lufthansa 37

M

Madinat Jumeirah 69
Madinat Theatre 196
Magnolia Bakery 213
Maison Bagatelle 275
Majlis Gallery 86, 184
Majlis Ghorfat Um Al Sheif 112
Mall of
  the Emirates 20, 121, 154, 205
Malls 27
Mamzar Beach Park 92
Man/Age 171
Mandara Spa 171
Mango Tree 195
Mangrove Forest 134
Manhattan Grill 276
Mannaland
  Korean Restaurant 276
Margaux 195
Marina Market 191
Marina Walk 103
Market Place, The 276
Marks & Spencer 213
Marsa Dubai 74, 102
Massage 166
Meat Co., The 277
Media 48

Medications 39
Meena Bazaar 197
Mercato 206
Mercato Mall 110
Mercure Grand
  Jebel Hafeet Hotel 133
Meridien Village Terrace 277
Metro 18, 54
Meydan Racecourse 18
Mini-golf 77
Mirdif City Centre 208
Modern Dubai 16, 17
Money 41
Monorail 56, 121
Montgomerie Golf Club 151
Moroccan Baths 166
Mosque Tours 112
Motorsport 152, 152, 162
Movies Under The Stars 226
Mubadala World
  Tennis Championship 165
Murooj 222
Musandam 138, 148, 158
Muscat 138
Museums 135, 137
Mutrah 138

N

N'Dulge Nightclub 311
Nail Bars 174
Nasimi Beach 278
National Car Rental 58
National Dress 14
National Museum
  of Ras Al Khaimah 136
Nawwara 278
Neos 311
Net Tours 142
  ...ADVERT 141

New Dubai	102, 121	Parasailing	158, 151	Religion	13
Newspapers & Magazines	48	Park Hyatt Dubai	70	Resort & Spa	69
Nezeasussi Grill	311	Pars Iranian Kitchen	282	Restaurants & Cafes	246
Nightclubs	223	Peace Rally	152	Ritz-Carlton	71,172
Nina	278	Penguins	97, 154	Ritz-Carlton Dubai International	
Nineteen	279	People & Economy	16	Financial Centre	72
Nobu	30, 117, 279	Peppercrab	284	Ritz-Carlton Spa	172
Nol Card	56, 57	Perfumes	194	Road & Transport	
Northern Emirates	136	Pier 7	202	Authority	57
NStyle Nail Lounge	174	Pierchic	284	Ronda Locatelli	288
Nuran Marina		Places To Stay	64	Rooftop Terrace	
Serviced Residences	74	Planetarium	122	& Sports Lounge, The	312
		Plant Street	128	Rostang	117
O		Police	44	Royal Brunei Airlines	37
Oasis Palm Tourism	142	Pride of Kashmir	186	Royal Jet	37
Observatory, The	280	Public Holidays &		Rugby	163
Oeno Wine Bar	312	Annual Events	50	Rugby Sevens	53, 163
Okku	280	Pubs & Clubs	300	Ruth's Chris Steak House	288
Old Dubai	74, 89				
Oman	138, 148, 158	Q		S	
Oman Air	37	Qatar Airways	37	Saadiyat Island	132
Omega Dubai		Quad bikes	164	Safa Park	113
Desert Classic	51, 161			Safari, Desert	140
Omeir Travel Agency	142	R		Sahn Eddar	117, 288
One&Only Private Spa	172	Radio	49	Saks Fifth Avenue	198, 214
One&Only Royal Mirage	69	Radisson Blu Hotel	75	Salalah	138
Opera Gallery	128, 184	Radisson Blu Resort	134	Salmontini Le Resto	289
Organic Glow		Raffles Dubai	70	Sanctuary Pool Lounge	312
Beauty Lounge	174	Rallying	152	Saravana Bhavan	194, 289
Orient Tours	142	Ramada Downtown Dubai	70	Saray Spa	173
Oriental Hammam	172	...ADVERT	73	Satori Spa	76
Ossiano	280	Ramadan	50	Satwa	188, 197, 223
		Ras Al Hadd Turtle Reserve	138	Scuba Diving	97
P		Ras Al Jinz	138	Seafire Steakhouse & Bar	289
Pachanga	282	Ras Al Khaimah	136	Seawings	140, 142
Pai Thai	282	Rashidiya	184	SEGA Republic	99, 202
Palace Downtown Dubai, The	70	Ravi's Restaurant	284	...ADVERT	IFC
Palladium	228	Reem Al Bawadi	285	Segreto	290
Palm Jumeirah	80, 116, 117	Reflets Par Pierre Gagnaire	286	SensAsia Urban Spa	115, 174

Service Charge	41	Skate	154
Shabestan	290	Ski Dubai	20, 154, 205, 250
Shades	313	...ADVERT	155
Shake	183	Skiing & Snowboarding	154
Shang Palace	290	SKY	21
Shangri-La	72	Skyview Bar	25, 117, 314
Sharaf DG	217	Snoopy Island	133
Sharjah Museum Department		Snow Park	154
...ADVERT	iv, v	Snowboarding	154
Sharjah Natural History &		Souk Al Arsah	137
Botanical Museum	137	Souk	
Shawarma	224	Al Bahar	29, 34, 185, 195, 204
Sheikh Mohammed Centre for		Souk Madinat	
Cultural Understanding	111	Jumeirah	118, 184, 195
Sheikh Rashid bin Saeed		Souks	182
Al Maktoum	112	Souks & Markets	190
Sheikh Saeed		South African Airways	37
Al Maktoum House	86	Souvenirs	194, 187
Sheikh Zayed		Spa At	
Grand Mosque	130	Hilton Dubai	174
Sheikh Zayed Road	64, 96	Jumeirah, The	174
Shell Festival Parade	152	Spa At The Address	175
Sheraton Dubai	71	Spa at Shangri-La, The	175
Sheraton Dubai Creek		Spa At The Palace, The	101
Hotel & Towers	74	Spas	166
Shimal	137	Spectator Sports	160
Shipping	183	Spectrum On One	291
Shisha	13, 224	Spice Souk	24, 90, 93, 196
Sho Cho	313	Splendido Restaurant	291
Shooting	77	Spring Desert Rally (4WD)	152
Shopping	128	Street Food	224
Shopping Malls	198	Sultan's Lounge	292
Siddharta Lounge		Sumibiya	292
By Buddha Bar	313	Sunflower Tours	142
Signature By		Supermarkets	
Sanjeev Kapoor	286	& Hypermarkets	214
Singapore Airlines	37	Sur Mer	293
Six Senses Zighy Bay	134	Surf	159
Sizing	182		

T			
Table 9	293		
Tagine	293		
Tailoring	188		
Talise	118		
Talise Spa	121, 176		
Taste of Home	294		
Taxi	56, 60		
Telephone & Internet	46		
Television	49		
Tennis	77, 165		
Terrace, The	314		
Textile Souk	24, 84, 197		
Thai Kitchen, The	107, 294		
Third Line, The	33, 129		
Theatre	228		
The Beach at Jumeirah			
Beach Residence	103		
Theme parks	132		
Thiptara	294		
Thrifty Car Rental	58		
Time	40		
Tipping	41		
Tips & Toes	174		
Tokyo@thetowers	295		
Toro Toro	295		
Tour Dubai	142		
Tour Operators	142		
Tourism	18		
Tours & Sightseeing	140, 142		
Trader Vic's	295		
Trader Vic's Mai-Tai Lounge	314		
Traiteur	296		
Tram	18		
Travco	142		
Troyka	296		
Trucial Coast	6		
Turtles	148		

U

UAE Desert Challenge	162
Umm Al Quwain	136
Umm Hurair	122
Underground Pub, The	315
Underwater Zoo	97
United Airlines	37
Uptown Bar	316

V

Vegetarian Food	222
Villa Beach	296
Villas	75
Virgin Atlantic	37
Visa	38, 39
Visiting Dubai	36
Voda Bar	316

W

Wadi & Dune Bashing	156
Wadi Adventure	133, 159
Wadis	156
Wafi	32, 122, 210, 185
Wagamama	297
Walk, The	209, 246
Walking	62
Warehouse	316
Water Park	132
Water Bus	63
Watersports	77, 137, 158, 156
Wavebreaker	317
West 14th
New York Grill & Bar	297
Wheelchair Access	45
White Water Rafting	159
White X Beach
& Lounge	317
Wild Wadi Water Park	34, 118
...ADVERT	ix

Windsurfing	158
Wonder Bus Tours	26, 142

X

XVA Art Hotel	75
XVA Gallery	87

Y

Yalumba	297
Yas Beach	132
Yas Island	152, 165
...ADVERT	ii, iii
Yas Links Golf Club	132
Yas Marina Circuit	132, 152, 165
Yas Viceroy	132
Yas Waterworld	132
...ADVERT	x, IBC
Yo! Sushi	298

Z

Zabeel Park	123
Zafran	298
Zheng He's	118, 298
Zinc	317
Zuma	101, 299

Explorer Products

Check out ask**explorer**.com/shop

Residents' Guides

Visitors' Guides

Photography Books & Calendars

Maps & Atlases

Adventure & Lifestyle Guides

Apps & eBooks

+ Also available as applications.
Visit askexplorer.com/apps.

* Now available in eBook format.

Visit **askexplorer.com/shop** for our full product list.

For bulk orders and customised copies, go to **askexplorer.com/corporate**

explorer

Explorer Team

Publishing
Chief Content Officer & Founder
Alistair MacKenzie

Editorial
Sr. Corporate Editor Julie Hayes
Editor Lisa Crowther, Kirsty Tuxford
Research Manager Mimi Stankova
Researchers Amrit Raj, Roja P, Praseena,
Shalu Sukumar, Maria Luisa Reyes,
Lara Santizo, Jacqueline Reyes
Production Coordinator
Joy Viernes

Design & Photography
Art Director Ieyad Charaf
Layout Manager Jayde Fernandes
Designer M. Shakkeer, Mohamed Abdo
Junior Designer Niyasuthin Batcha
Cartography Manager Zain Madathil
Cartographer Noushad Madathil, Ramla
Kambravan, Jithesh Kalathingal
GIS Analyst Jobydas KD, Aslam
Photographer & Image Editor
Hardy Mendrofa

Sales
Director of Sales Peter Saxby
Media Sales Area Managers
Laura Zuffa, Sabrina Ahmed, Bryan Anes,
Simon Reddy, Sean Rutherford
Digital Sales Manager Rola Touffaha

Business Development Manager
Pouneh Hafizi
Director of Retail Ivan Rodrigues
Retail Sales Coordinator
Michelle Mascarenhas
Retail Sales Area Supervisors
Ahmed Mainodin, Firos Khan
Retail Sales Merchandisers Johny Mathew,
Shan Kumar, Mehmood Ullah
Retail Sales Drivers Shabsir Madathil,
Nimicias Arachchige
Warehouse Assistant Mohamed Haji,
Jithinraj M

Finance, HR & Administration
Accountant Cherry Enriquez
Accounts Assistants Sunil Suvarna,
Jayleen Aguinaldo
Administration Joy San Buenaventura
Reception Jayfee Manseguiao
Delivery Driver & PRO Imran Mhalunkar
Office Assistant Shafeer Ahamed
Office Manager – India Jithesh Kalathingal

IT & Digital Solutions
Web Developers Mirza Ali Nasrullah,
Waqas Razzaq
HTML/UI Developer Naveed Ahmed
IT Manager R. Ajay
Database Programmer Pradeep T.P.

How Can We Help You?

Ask Explorer   ask**explorer**.com
Log onto our new website for information, event listings and
competitions in your city and other places across the Middle East.

Media Sales   sales@ask**explorer**.com
Contact us for details of our advertising rates, corporate bulk
sales, online marketing packages, content licensing and
customised wall maps.

Corporate Sales   corporate@ask**explorer**.com
For all your corporate needs, Explorer services include bulk sales
orders, mapping solutions, corporate gifts, bespoke publications,
customised dust jackets and a wide range of digital options.

Retail Sales   retail@ask**explorer**.com
Check out Explorer retail sales options, distribution services and
E-shop orders.

General Enquiries   info@ask**explorer**.com
Call us on +971 (0)4 340 8805 as we'd love to hear your thoughts
and answer any questions you might have about this book or any
Explorer products.

Careers   jobs@ask**explorer**.com
Send us your CV if you are talented, adventurous,
knowledgeable, curious, passionate, creative and above all fun.

Useful Numbers

Dubai Municipality	04 221 5555/800 900
Tourist Security Department	800 4438
Dubai Police (Emergency)	999
Fire Department	997
Ambulance	999/998
American Hospital	04 336 7777
Medcare Hospital	04 407 9111
Life Pharmacy (24 Hour)	04 344 1122
UAE Country Code	+971
Dubai Area Code	04
Directory Enquiries	181/199
International Operator Assistance	100
Weather Updates	04 216 2218

Airport Info

Emirates Airline	600 55 55 55
flydubai	231 1000
Dubai International Airport:	
Help Desk	04 224 5555
Flight Information	04 224 5555
Baggage Services	04 224 5383
Dubai World Central Airport:	
Headquarters	04 814 1111

Taxi Companies

Arabia Taxis	04 285 5566
Dubai Taxi	04 208 0808
Cars Taxis	800 227 789
Metro Taxis	600 566 000
National Taxis	600 543 322